PRAISE FOR *LOVE HER WELL*

"Kari Kampakis is a voice I trust when it comes to parenting a teen girl, not because she's the mom of four girls but because she's a praying mom of four girls. She would be the first to tell you that any wisdom she has to offer is because God has shown her the way. *Love Her Well* is the book every mom of a teen girl should read and underline and keep on her bedside table. These are the parenting years when we have to walk the tightrope of holding on and letting go all at the same time, and Kari has given us a guide to do it in a way that honors these precious girls that have been entrusted to us. If raising a teenage girl feels scary, it's because it absolutely can be. Fortunately, Kari has written an incredibly helpful guide to help us not just to survive these years, but to equip us be the best version of ourselves."

—Melanie Shankle, *New York Times* bestselling author of
On the Bright Side and co-host of *The Big Boo Cast*

"Here's what I will tell you about *Love Her Well*: it is the best book I have ever read about the mother-daughter dynamic. If that sounds like high praise, it's because it is. Kari's transparency and vulnerability in these pages will minister to moms regardless of their girls' ages and give them a safe place to process their struggles and their victories. With words that are patient, understanding, and full of grace, *Love Her Well* will be a patient companion for the mom who is overwhelmed, frustrated, or constantly asking herself, *Am I doing this right? Am I doing this well?* Kari's deep affection for both moms and daughters is so evident, so life-giving, and I will recommend this book over and over again. I don't often say that a book is going to change people's lives, but this one will. It is absolutely needed, and it is absolutely beautiful."

—Sophie Hudson, author of *Stand All the Way Up*
and co-host of *The Big Boo Cast*

"For years, Kari Kampakis has been one of my most trusted sources to speak truth into the lives of teenage girls, with her trademark warm, humble, honest, affirming voice. I am delighted she is now speaking directly to the hearts of moms, offering that same truth in ways that will not only connect but help them love their girls with understanding, with strength, and with hope. Please buy a copy of this book for yourself and for the moms you know who are doing their best to love their girls well. You, your friends, and your girls will be glad you did!"

—Sissy Goff, M.Ed., LPC-MHSP, Director of Child & Adolescent Counseling, Daystar Counseling Ministries and author of eleven books, including *Raising Worry-Free Girls*

"Kari has done something wonderful here. Sharing stories, personal experiences, and essential truths, she has illuminated and prioritized what matters most in raising strong, caring girls. As a mom of three boys, I could relate because these principles are universal. I love this book on so many levels, and since parenting teenagers has never been harder, it comes at exactly the right time."

—Dr. Michele Borba, author of *UnSelfie* and *Thrivers: The Surprising Reasons Why Some Kid Struggle and Others Shine*

"We've all heard the popular saying 'to know her is to love her,' but these words have never come to life quite the way they do in *Love Her Well*. In it, Kari Kampakis demonstrates a unique and profound understanding of the teen-girl world, including what they need most from moms. Kari is a master at shedding light on how adults can do the vital work of raising girls who live out their God-given purposes bravely, boldly, flawed, and full of hope. Not only will our daughters be more content as a result of reading *Love Her Well*, but so will we."

—Rachel Macy Stafford, *New York Times* bestselling author, speaker, and certified special education teacher

"I call Kari Kampakis the Daughter Whisperer. And as a mom of two teenage daughters, I'm going to read anything this woman writes. I trust Kari for her proven track record in helping moms and daughters connect, relate, and live into their God-given identities. Kari does it again with *Love Her Well*. This book is a must-read for any mom who wants more than to simply *survive* the teen years. This is a book for anyone who wants to see their mom-daughter relationship truly *thrive*."

—Jennifer Dukes Lee, author of *It's All Under Control*

"With compassion and insights, *Love Her Well* sheds lights on the important and often complex topic of building relationships with our daughters. Kari Kampakis's vulnerability empowers parents to understand they're not alone, as her own experiences provide wisdom and skills to navigate raising a teenager. This is a must-read book, and most importantly—a book to share with a friend who has a daughter."

—Sue Scheff, author of *Shame Nation: The Global Epidemic of Online Hate*

"Having written two acclaimed books for teen girls, Kari is already a trusted voice among mothers of daughters. It's no surprise that Kari is now empowering moms to lead and love their daughters well. In *Love Her Well*, Kari writes in her familiar 'me too' voice and offers invaluable wisdom for creating and keeping a grace-filled relationship with your daughter."

—Jeannie Cunnion, author of *Mom Set Free*

"As a mom to four boys, I may be the biggest fan you'll find of *Love Her Well*. I had tears in my eyes in every single chapter as I felt such security knowing that Kari Kampakis is offering biblical values and hard-earned wisdom to mothers of girls today. On behalf of boy moms everywhere, I highly endorse this beautifully written book packed with practical ideas, relatable humor, and so much hope."

—Monica Swanson, author of *Boy Mom* and host of the *Boy Mom* podcast

"I love this book! As the mother of two teenage daughters, I feel like I don't know how to connect with them as easily as I once did, and I'm constantly on the lookout for insightful teachings that can show new ways to connect and grow our relationship. This book has that and more. I can't wait to get a group of moms together to read it."

—Emily West, mom of two girls, wife of
Christian artist Matthew West

"Parenting teens has never been more challenging, and adolescent girls are experiencing depression and anxiety at record-setting levels. *Love Her Well* is an absolute lifeline for parents who worry that they aren't doing it right or who are experiencing tension with their daughter. Filled with practical help, spiritual encouragement, and inspirational stories, Kari offers us a guidebook for the teen years. This is not a book you will put on your shelf; rather, you will turn to it over and over again!"

—Krista Gilbert, author of *Reclaiming Home*, speaker, home
coach, and co-host of *The Open Door Sisterhood* podcast

"As a big fan of Kari's writings and blog, I was so excited to hear she had another book in the works! This book does not disappoint . . . if flagged pages and highlighted text are indicators of a good, helpful, and relevant book with implementable strategies, then *Love Her Well* hits the mark. I am thankful Kari is willing to share her gift to benefit mothers and daughters."

—Whitney Long, co-founder of The Southern Coterie

LOVE HER WELL

10 WAYS TO FIND JOY AND CONNECTION
WITH YOUR TEENAGE DAUGHTER

KARI KAMPAKIS

W PUBLISHING GROUP

AN IMPRINT OF THOMAS NELSON

Published in Nashville, Tennessee, by W Publishing, an imprint of Thomas Nelson.

Published in association with the literary agency of Wolgemuth & Associates, Inc.

Thomas Nelson titles may be purchased in bulk for educational, business, fund-raising, or sales promotional use. For information, please e-mail SpecialMarkets@ThomasNelson.com.

Unless otherwise noted, Scripture quotations are taken from the Holy Bible, New International Version®, NIV®. Copyright © 1973, 1978, 1984, 2011 by Biblica, Inc.® Used by permission of Zondervan. All rights reserved worldwide. www.Zondervan.com. The "NIV" and "New International Version" are trademarks registered in the United States Patent and Trademark Office by Biblica, Inc.®

Scripture quotations marked ESV are taken from the ESV® Bible (The Holy Bible, English Standard Version®), copyright © 2001 by Crossway, a publishing ministry of Good News Publishers. Used by permission. All rights reserved.

Scripture quotations marked NLT are taken from the Holy Bible, New Living Translation. © 1996, 2004, 2007, 2013, 2015 by Tyndale House Foundation. Used by permission of Tyndale House Publishers, Inc., Carol Stream, Illinois 60188. All rights reserved.

Scripture quotations marked THE MESSAGE are taken from *The Message*. Copyright © by Eugene H. Peterson 1993, 1994, 1995, 1996, 2000, 2001, 2002. Used by permission of NavPress. All rights reserved. Represented by Tyndale House Publishers, Inc.

Any Internet addresses, phone numbers, or company or product information printed in this book are offered as a resource and are not intended in any way to be or to imply an endorsement by Thomas Nelson, nor does Thomas Nelson vouch for the existence, content, or services of these sites, phone numbers, companies, or products beyond the life of this book.

ISBN 978-0-7852-3419-7 (eBook)

Library of Congress Cataloging-in-Publication Data is on file.

ISBN 978-0-7852-3418-0

Printed in the United States of America

23 24 25 26 27 LBC 26 25 24 23 22

To my mom, whose dream to be a writer sparked my dream to be a writer. In your final season on earth, you taught me unforgettable life lessons about resiliency and grace. I love you, and I hope I inherit your heroic inner strength and kind spirit.

And to my girls: Ella, Sophie, Marie Claire, and Camille. You are the game-changers, the ones who launched me into the deep end of love, and it is through my heart for you that I share these words with other families raising girls.

10 WAYS TO FIND JOY AND CONNECTION WITH YOUR TEENAGE DAUGHTER

1. Choose your words (and timing) carefully.
2. Listen and empathize with her world.
3. Be her mom.
4. Make your relationship a priority.
5. See the good, loving her *as* she is and *where* she is.
6. Help her find good friends and positive influences.
7. Be her emotional coach.
8. Enjoy her, laugh often, and have fun.
9. Take care of yourself and have a support system for hard days.
10. Pray for her and empower her through faith.

CONTENTS

Note from the Author   XIII

Introduction   XVII

Chapter 1: Choose Your Words (and Timing) Carefully   1

Chapter 2: Listen and Empathize with Her World   17

Chapter 3: Be Her Mom   38

Chapter 4: Make Your Relationship a Priority   69

Chapter 5: See the Good, Loving Her *as* She Is
                and *Where* She Is   92

Chapter 6: Help Her Find Good Friends and
                Positive Influences   111

Chapter 7: Be Her Emotional Coach   130

Chapter 8: Enjoy Her, Laugh Often, and Have Fun   146

Chapter 9: Take Care of Yourself and Have a Support
                System for Hard Days   160

Chapter 10: Pray for Her and Empower Her Through Faith   180

Conclusion   193

Acknowledgments   197

Notes   203

About the Author   211

NOTE FROM THE AUTHOR

During the prelaunch of this book, my mother passed away. I knew it was a possibility because her health trials had grown intense. Still, I dreamed of her being at my book signings, smiling proudly and cheering me on. This message—about the deep, special, and intricate bond between mothers and daughters—was one I was especially excited to share with my mom. After all, she helped shape the story line.

My mom wasn't perfect, but she was the perfect mom for me and our family. She was externally gentle and internally tough, a quintessential Steel Magnolia. Growing up, I never bought into the stereotype of women being mean, gossipy, or ultracritical because that's not what I saw modeled. My mom was warm, kind, friendly, compassionate, and smart. She loved her friends, and they loved her back.

Our hearts broke as hospice told us that we only had a few days left with my mom. Overcome with emotion, my siblings and I searched her office for photos and mementos. I thought I knew my mother, yet hours later, after sifting through random keepsakes—for example, prayers for her five children, a stack of blog posts from my website, my brother's ninth-grade essay, a journal from her 2007 battle with cancer, and more—I realized my perspective was limited. I'd spend the rest of my life learning my mother's story.

I'm the fourth child in my family, and my sister Krissie is the fifth. We both inherited Mom's love for writing (Krissie teaches high school English), and my mother often joked that our careers began on her office floor. After picking us up from school, she'd take us to her workplace, and when we complained about being bored, she'd hand us paper and pens and tell us to get creative.

It worked, and after retirement, as my mom pursued her dream of being an author, she invited Krissie and me to join her at writing conferences. These classes were the kick that I needed, and after my mother self-published her memoir, I decided to write a book. If she could do it, maybe I could too.

My mother died in February 2020, and on the third morning after we lost her, it occurred to me how February is the month of love. How fitting. Even though I missed her deep in my bones, and I knew that ache would exist until I saw her again in heaven, I found peace in knowing that God brought her home during a season of love.

In short, my mother *was* love. Every decision she made—from choosing our family home, to setting aside paychecks to start a wedding fund for her daughters, to taking off two weeks from work when I had mono to nurse me back to health, to making Greek salads for my Greek husband when he visited, to never missing a birthday party for her fifteen grandchildren—was rooted in love.

I wish I'd realized the depth of her love while she was alive, but the beauty of my mom was that she didn't seek recognition. She just loved quietly and unconditionally, giving her heart freely without strings or motives attached.

My mom is my reminder to love my daughters like God loves us. Even when the relationship feels one-sided, even when I feel underappreciated, I can faithfully stay the course. You can too. One day our daughters will feel the pain that I feel now, yet if our earthly relationship ends in a good place, they'll also feel peace and gratitude. They'll smile as they remember their best memories with Mom.

More than ever, I believe in the mother-daughter relationship. I understand how nothing in this world can replace a mother or a mother's love. Your imprint in your daughter's life runs deep and wide, and rather than let that intimidate you, let it inspire you. Every silent sacrifice, every small act of love, every prayer you pray on your knees—it all matters. None of us will ever be perfect moms, but with willing hearts and help from above, we can be the moms our daughters need.

In Christ,
Kari

INTRODUCTION

Show them love, and they will listen
to your words of wisdom.
–DR. GARY CHAPMAN, *THE 5 LOVE
LANGUAGES OF TEENAGERS*[1]

My husband found me on the closet floor, crying like a baby.
I'd hit a rock-bottom mama moment, and I couldn't catch
my breath to explain what was wrong.

He knew nothing about my struggle because I'd kept it to
myself. I honestly thought it would pass. For months my then
thirteen-year-old daughter and I had been locking horns, and the
tension between us was continuing to escalate.

That morning before school, we fought again. She stormed
out the front door, and though I considered apologizing for losing
my temper, I held back because of pride.

After all, it was *her attitude* causing our problems. *Her moodiness* and *her sass* were changing our once-loving dynamic. If
anyone needed to change, it was *her*, not me.

Everyone had warned me about the teenage years, and now their predictions were coming true. The only way to navigate this new teen territory, I assured myself, was to dig in my heels and firmly take control. Otherwise, this daughter and her three sisters would walk all over me.

Yet an hour later, in the peace of a quiet home, I regretted that morning's fight and every silly fight before it. *What kind of mother yells at her child without owning up to it and making amends before she leaves? What if a tragedy occurred that day and my last words to my daughter were hostile and harsh?*

I hated how coldly I'd been acting toward her, and as that truth sank in, as I quit making excuses for why she needed a firm reprimand, I fell to my knees in my closet, begging God to help me restore our rocky relationship.

My husband heard my breakdown and came to comfort me. Thankfully, he was working from home that day, and he waited patiently for me to share what I'd been wrestling with inside.

> *I feel like I'm losing our daughter, and I don't know what to do.*
>
> *Deep down, I worry that I'm jeopardizing our relationship in some irrevocable way. I feel a big pressure to get it right because if ever there was a time when I want us to be close, it is now, in middle school, when not feeling loved or understood at home might make her more easily swayed by peer pressure.*
>
> *She is changing, and so is our relationship, and what used to work no longer does. What I can't figure out is how to balance loving her with parenting her. How do I correct the attitudes and behavior I don't like while keeping a strong mother-daughter connection?*

It felt good to be honest, and though my husband and I could not immediately solve the problem, I realized a few things when I admitted my struggle.

One, I missed my close relationship with my daughter and the easy rapport we shared.

Two, I needed a new approach to parenting her, one that didn't widen the gulf between us with every disagreement.

And three, if I wanted to reconnect with her, I had to take the lead. For teenagers, engaging with parents isn't a top priority. My daughter would never come to me and say, "Mom, I wish we were closer. It bothers me that we're not."

My breakdown on the closet floor was my wake-up call. It was when I finally admitted that my daughter was growing up, and that our relationship had to grow up too. To remain part of her life in this new season we'd entered, I needed to bridge the gap between her heart and mine.

This is what inspired my search for how to love a teenage daughter.

———————————— • ————————————

Love is patient and kind. Love is not jealous or boastful or proud or rude.

–1 CORINTHIANS 13:4 NLT

———————————— • ————————————

GOD CHOSE YOU

Before you move on, please repeat this:

I won't waste time beating myself up.

I won't dwell on regret.

I will remember that I am loved.

I started this book with a mom fail to assure you that you're not alone. We all struggle and fall flat on our face at times. By raising my hand to say, "Okay, I'll go first. I'll admit what has happened in my own home," I hope you'll feel safe enough to do the same.

The truth is, a mother's confidence is fragile. Despite any bravado or outward appearance that we have our act together, it takes only one glitch, fight, or failure to trigger our deepest insecurities.

Even the most epic high can suddenly come crashing down with one mistake . . . one argument . . . one comment we wish to retract.

The good news is, we serve a mighty God. He is the only One who ultimately matters. God chose *you* to be your daughter's mother, and since God doesn't make mistakes, you can be confident in His decision even when you lose confidence in yourself.

There is strength in vulnerability and freedom in telling your daughter that you're not perfect, but Jesus is—and the goal is to be like Him. Together you two can grow and learn, letting God transform you with a strength of spirit and a tender, responsive heart (Ezekiel 36:26).

Your teenage daughter faces unprecedented challenges. She needs strong women in her life who can guide her, encourage her, and protect her. Women who add wind to her sails and speak truth into her soul when her inner critic gets loud. Women who acknowledge the harsh realities of this world and turn to the comforting truths of the Bible.

God's mercies are new every morning, and rather than spending today lamenting the past or worrying about the future, I encourage you to accept God's present grace. *Let your Father love you as you love your daughter.*

God desires a relationship with each of you, and as you build new bridges and knock down old walls between you and your daughter, I pray you come to realize how known, valued, and deeply loved you are.

---●---

All glory to God, who is able, through his mighty power at work within us, to accomplish infinitely more than we might ask or think.

—EPHESIANS 3:20 NLT

---●---

TO BE HONEST...

I almost didn't write this book. Even as words and ideas took shape, I had serious reservations.

After all, I'm not a parenting expert. I mess up all the time. I believe my best advice will come in twenty years, when my four daughters are grown adults and I have the broader perspective that only time can bring.

But I wrote this book because moms are struggling *now*. Moms want to hear from other moms who are in the foxhole with them and "get" their secret battles. In twenty years, our parenting culture will look totally different, and though I may have more wisdom, I won't relate to those parents like I can relate to parents today.

This book is also an act of obedience. I know that God wants me to share my stories and resources, but within weeks of starting this manuscript, new tensions arose between me and one daughter. As my inner critic screamed, *Who do you think you are to write this? You're totally unqualified!*, I realized I had a choice. I could either quit and accept defeat—or I could lean into my struggles and write from a place of vulnerability and deep trust in God.

As this book releases, I'll have three teenage daughters and one preteen daughter. I'll need the kinds of conversations that I hope this book inspires. While I have long had a heart for teen girls—and eagerly wrote two books for them—God has slowly softened my heart to the moms of teen girls as I became one myself.

Up front, I'd like to share what laid the groundwork for this message.

My Core Beliefs About Parenting

1. **God loves your daughter more than you do.** He has a great plan for her life *and* your life.
2. **Parenting is more challenging than ever before.** It is too big to handle alone, especially in the teen years.
3. **We have an enemy who seeks to steal, kill, and destroy (John 10:10).** He wants division in all your relationships—including the one with your daughter. The Greek word for devil is *diabolos*, and it means "the one who divides." Since the light of Christ overcomes all darkness, He is your ultimate protector.
4. **Your relationship with your daughter is as unique as your thumbprint.** You can't compare it to anyone else's relationship, but you can learn from other moms and find common ground in your journeys.
5. **Nobody is guaranteed tomorrow.** Life can change in a snap. Hug your loved ones, pick your battles, and don't let the sun go down on your anger.
6. **Every child is just one decision away from stupid,** one decision away from making you look like the *worst mother on earth*. Staying mindful of this keeps you humble and compassionate toward other parents.

7. **We are all sinners in need of grace and a Savior.** We have a merciful Father who forgives the sins we confess to Him and can use them for good. God's grace is bigger than any mistake or bad choice, and in the same way that He loves and forgives us, we're called to love and forgive each other.

8. **Negative thoughts lead your mind to dark places.** They make you parent out of fear, not love. God created you for more. He wants you to enjoy your daughter by growing deeply dependent on His wisdom, protection, and guidance.

9. **Together is better.** I recommend studying this book with a small group of women you trust and respect. Be careful to protect your daughter's privacy by sharing stories about you, not her. If she finds out you've shared too much about her, she'll shut down on you or possibly shut you out.

10. **Change begins with you.** This book is not a guide on how to "fix" your daughter or control her; instead, it offers insight on how to deepen your connection, stay strong, work through conflict, learn from your mistakes, and take care of yourself as your daughter becomes a young adult.

11. **Any relationship that lasts a long time will have ups and downs: good seasons, bad seasons, rewarding seasons, and dry seasons.** Your relationship with your daughter will never be perfect, but it can be exceptional.

12. **Your daughter needs you.** As her first love, you have a unique and life-altering influence on her, and a strong relationship with you can profoundly impact her life. I'm rooting for you both!

Parents love to commiserate over the agony of raising teenagers. Even when our kids are small, even as we snuggle with our newborn babies, we are warned that adolescence is a season to survive. While the challenges of adolescence are undeniably formidable, we miss a major opportunity to connect with our daughters when we settle for the world's gloomy narrative.

After all, teenagers are highly perceptive, and when they overhear us talking about what a pain they are—or see books on our nightstands with angsty adolescents and negative titles on the cover—it doesn't help the relationship.

Imagine how you'd feel if you walked into your daughter's room and saw a book on her nightstand titled *Dealing with a Difficult Mom*. It wouldn't exactly warm your heart, right?

Rather than say, "This is impossible," maybe we can say, "This requires effort, but my daughter is worth it." We love because God loved us first. We don't give up on our child because God doesn't give up on us.

In her book *Give Them Wings*, author Carol Kuykendall describes adolescence as a painful season with conflicting emotions. As your daughter tries to become a person who doesn't need you, you try to become a parent who accepts and encourages that independence. At the same time, you hold on to every moment because you don't want to let go.

I know parents who proudly proclaim, "Roots and wings, do great things!" as their children leave the nest. I also know parents who are emotional wrecks. Whichever camp you fall in, we can all benefit from Kuykendall's advice to *embrace* the home-stretch season of parenting by intentionally making the most of our time with our teenagers.

As Kuykendall points out, "The ultimate relationship we desire with our children—on the other side of this transition—is an adult-to-adult friendship that grows from the way we navigate and encourage their confident independence in their last years at home."[2]

Since this adult relationship could last thirty or forty years (far longer than a child's first eighteen years of life), it's worth considering the stage being set while our daughters are under our roof.

Again, I'm on this journey with you. I'm writing this book as a note to self. As C. S. Lewis said, "We have to be continually reminded of what we believe."[3] By sharing what I believe as a mom of girls and a writer for teen and tween girls, I hope you'll feel empowered, encouraged, and challenged to consider what is best for you and your family. I hope your connection with your daughter grows deeper than ever before as you love her well through the teenage years.

———————— • ————————

What then shall we say to these things? If God is for us, who can be against us?

—ROMANS 8:31 ESV

———————— • ————————

REFLECTION QUESTIONS

1. What happens to a mom's "village" as her children grow up? Why do moms feel supported in the toddler years yet lonely in the teen years?

2. When did you first notice signs of your daughter growing up? What was your response?

3. Have you and your daughter ever locked horns or hit a rough patch? If so, what helped you through it? In retrospect, what would you have done differently?

4. What positive or negative scripts about raising girls have you heard? How have they shaped your parenting?

5. Do you live in the past (beating yourself up over mistakes), the present (accepting God's current grace), or the future (worrying about what's ahead)? How would your outlook change if you woke up believing God's mercies are new each morning?

6. Describe your relationship with your mother. In what ways has it positively or negatively impacted the way you relate to and interact with your daughter?

. . . .

1

CHOOSE YOUR WORDS (AND TIMING) CAREFULLY

Criticism is the number one killer
of relationships. Period.
—ALICE CHURNOCK[1]

My daughter and I had an amazing conversation in the car. The words flowed easily, and so did the laughter. It was a gorgeous fall day, and as I drove down streets lined with trees and leaves in every autumn shade, the world felt right. My daughter and I sang along with Adele and talked about life and growing up. I felt especially close to her, and I could tell she felt the same.

As I parked in the driveway, I glanced at her in the passenger seat. I savored the high of our connection. Then, out of the blue, my thoughts suddenly shifted as the sunlight on her face highlighted an area of concern.

Her acne was back—looking flared up and red.

I opened my mouth to ask if she'd taken her acne medication, but something stopped me. I think it was God, telling me not to go there. Now was not the time, and being direct was not the way.

Months earlier when I asked this same question during another breakout, my daughter's face fell as she answered, "Yes, I'm taking it. I know my face looks terrible." She was aware of the issue, she was using her creams, and she didn't need my reminder. Her acne had become a sensitive subject, and after multiple trips to the dermatologist, we were still searching for the best remedy.

When my daughter got out of the car still happy from our time together, I knew I'd made the right choice. By holding my tongue, I didn't ruin the moment or undo the bonding that happened during our car ride.

I've ruined other moments, though, by blurting out thoughts. I've spoken carelessly and bluntly and seen the hurt reactions on my daughters' faces. I've expressed observations that were better left unsaid and failed to consider the timing and tone of my delivery.

With family members, it's easy to get lazy. Since we're comfortable around our family (and secure in feeling loved and safe), we're more likely to push limits and speak freely. Even if we stay on our best behavior for the world, when we get home, we drop our guards and relax our filters.

While most of us would never intentionally hurt our daughters, we often use language that is more hurtful than helpful. Words have power, and the words we speak as moms hold superpowers. With girls—who don't forget what's said to them—words can wreck a relationship.

Your daughter cares deeply about your opinions of her. She takes your words to heart, and regardless of her demeanor as you're talking, your voice resonates louder than others.

In his book *Whisper*, pastor Mark Batterson notes that by

the seventh month of pregnancy, a baby in utero recognizes and responds with specific muscular movements to his or her mother's voice. "Neuroimaging has also shown that a mother's voice exerts a unique influence, over and above a stranger's voice, by activating the reward circuits in the brain, as well as the amygdalae, which regulate emotion," he writes. "Simply put, a mother's voiceprint leaves a neural fingerprint that imprints her baby's brain."[2]

Even if you adopted your daughter or came into her life at a later time, your voice is like a megaphone due to the primary position you hold.

Being a mom requires difficult conversations that nobody has a script for. There is ample room for error as you find the right verbiage, tone, and timing. Ask anyone who has parented long enough—and who is honest—and they'll have stories of hurtful or untimely remarks they've made.

The goal, I believe, is to speak the truth in love. To figure out what needs to be said and find the best way and time to say it. This sounds simple, yet it's not, and only with prayer and God's guidance can we become moms who are wise with our words and effective in our approach.

---•---

"Now go! I will be with you as you speak, and I will instruct you in what to say."

—EXODUS 4:12 NLT

---•---

WHAT PLAYS ON REPEAT IN YOUR DAUGHTER'S HEAD?

One of the best parts of writing for both teen girls and their mothers is that I meet a broad spectrum of girl moms.

Moms who reach out to me all have these things in common: They love their daughters passionately. They desire a strong relationship, have a heart for their struggles, and want to offer wise counsel.

I learn a lot from these women, and I've had countless aha! moments during our conversations. One mom in Louisiana hit the nail on the head when she said this: "Our girls have the world telling them what's wrong with them. They need mamas who tell them what's right with them."

Wow. What truth. I liked this mom even more when she admitted to going through a rough patch with her teenage daughter. One night as her daughter questioned her love, this mother told her daughter, "I want you to sit in this chair before bed, and I'm going to tell you everything I think is right about you."

Too often we forget to say what's right. Especially in the teen years—when we're constantly teaching lessons, laying out rules, worrying about the future, and questioning our children's love for *us* as they talk back or act defiant—we get stuck in a negative loop. When they pull back, we pull back. Our instinct is to protect our hearts and show them who's the boss.

None of this grows the relationship. If anything, it deepens the divide and fosters hidden resentment.

This negative loop also affects self-image. As family counselor Sissy Goff explains, our words as parents set the course for how our children will see themselves for years to come. "In offices throughout the world," Goff writes, "counselors and therapists talk about the 'tapes' we hear in our heads, filling us with self-doubt. It is often the voices of our parents that make up those tapes."[3]

Frankly, I'd be a little scared to hear my daughters' unabridged tapes. Like all parents, I've done some things right and some things wrong. I've spoken out of my wounds, not my wisdom, too many times to count.

Don't use foul or abusive language. Let everything you
say be good and helpful, so that your words will be an
encouragement to those who hear them.

—EPHESIANS 4:29 NLT

HOW MY WORDS HURT MY DAUGHTER

Remember the opening story about me crying on my closet floor
after my daughter and I had locked horns?

What I didn't mention is how we worked through it—or what
led to our tension.

Before our rough patch, I'd read articles about teenagers and
hormones, how kids turn into Dr. Jekyll and Mr. Hyde, yet as
we celebrated my daughter's thirteenth birthday, none of them
applied. My sweet little girl was still my sweet little girl.

But in the spring of her seventh-grade year, our dynamic
shifted. She started sporting more attitude and distancing herself from me.

Looking back, I realize that inner turmoil was suddenly
rocking her world. That spring was hard for my daughter for
three reasons:

1. Hormones were kicking in—and so were the normal
   changes of adolescence.
2. Her grandfather died on New Year's Eve, which left her
   deeply sad.
3. Her best friend moved to a new city.

Her once stable world suddenly felt unstable, cultivating the
perfect storm.

After my closet-floor breakdown, I went to the gym and saw a close friend. I asked her how she handles fights with her daughter. She shared great advice.

"After an argument," she said, "you've got to circle back around. Go back when you're calm and have had time to think. Apologize, talk it out, and try to do better next time."

I apologized that afternoon, and I told my daughter how sad I'd been about all our recent fighting. She admitted that she'd been sad too. I asked if I'd done anything to upset her, and I expected her to say no, but she didn't.

Instead, she told me I'd become more critical and harder to please. This threw me for a loop and felt like a punch in the gut. At the same time, I knew she was right; I *had* become more critical. During this time, I'd become extracritical of myself, and I was projecting that onto her. I'd also pressured her with higher expectations as she was a newly minted middle schooler.

It took me a few days to own up to my mistakes, but taking accountability turned our relationship around. It also taught me a valuable lesson: teenagers respect honesty. They're okay with a parent who's not perfect, but they're not okay with a parent who acts perfect and tries to shift all the blame onto them.

William Barclay said, "If we find ourselves becoming critical of other people, we should stop examining them, and start examining ourselves."[4] I believe a critical spirit is the number one cause of tension between mothers and daughters. It's important to keep it in check and be aware of the blind spots that can impact our parenting, such as:

- being a control freak,
- thinking we're always right,
- being too prideful or stubborn to apologize,

- losing our temper,
- letting fear and anxiety drive our choices,
- not listening, and
- underestimating the impact of our words.

My daughter felt the pang of my criticism months after the fact. Although it hurt to hear this, I'd take that disappointment any day to work toward reconciliation with my child. Soon after, for Mother's Day, she handed me a book from her seventh-grade creative writing class. Her teacher had the students write about their families, and my heart stopped when I saw this:

"I can't wait until I can be a mother, and I hope my children love me as much as I love my mom."

After months of worrying about our relationship, I needed this reminder. I needed hope that I hadn't yelled my way straight out of her life. This book was a gift from God, and as I cried over my daughter's reflections, the happy memories she'd made with her family, friends, and even her sisters, I realized she'd had a great childhood despite any missteps on my part.

Have open communication with your daughter about your relationship. Be strong, and allow her to respectfully share her feelings without fear of hurting your feelings or getting in trouble. Humble yourself, swallow your pride, and ask God to examine your heart. If things are good, accept my virtual high five, and if not, accept my virtual hug of hope because today is the day you start turning things around.

"In your anger do not sin": Do not let the sun go down while you are still angry.

–EPHESIANS 4:26

SPEAK LIFE

If I suddenly had to choose only one audience to write for—adults or teenagers—I would choose teenagers.

Why? Because they're easier to influence. They are moldable in ways that adults are not.

I learned this while writing an article on teenage depression. At the time, I was blogging for parents, but during my interview with a doctor, she stirred in me a desire to help a younger audience.

"The reason I love working with children and teenagers," she told me, "is because they're so resilient. You can change the whole trajectory of their lives. Early intervention is key. It's a lot easier to intervene effectively when they're young instead of years later, when they've been depressed for so long that the illness becomes incorporated into their identity."

In short, adults are hard to change. We're more set in our ways, beliefs, habits, and mindsets. Children and teenagers, on the other hand, are still forming their identities and mindsets. They are what parenting experts often refer to as "wet cement."

Geri Scazzero, in her book *The Emotionally Healthy Woman*, expands on the concept of wet cement. "In our young and formative years," she writes, "we are like liquid cement into which our families leave deep, unconscious imprints. Those imprints eventually harden and are not easily changed. Only as we grow older do we realize the depth of their influence."[5]

Right now you have a unique window of opportunity with your daughter. Her concrete is still wet; her heart and mind are open. She is being deeply influenced by people, words, and events. As she grows up, her cement will harden. These early impressions will solidify and affect her self-perception and worldview.

We all want healthy daughters, and it's worth considering the marks we make as we handle the tough tasks of parenting, like

Punishment.

Discipline.

Consequences.

Correction.

Guidance.

Boundaries and rules.

Knowing how to parent in godly ways isn't always clear-cut. We may modify our kids' behavior, but if we petrify them or lead them to believe that they're only lovable when they act the way we expect, then we've failed as parents.

We won't reflect the very essence of Jesus: mercy and grace.

In Ephesians 4:15, we're instructed to speak the truth in love. In Proverbs 18:21, we're told that the tongue has the power of life and death. What does this mean? How do we disciple and discipline teenagers in a way that builds their spirit and helps them become healthy adults?

The starting point is to have God's Spirit inside us. His Spirit enables us to hear Him and recognize good parenting patterns being modeled by others that we can adopt into our lives.

Following are statements, questions, and words to encourage your daughter.

Thirty-Five Ways to Speak Life to a Teenager

1. How can I pray for you this week?
2. You can do hard things. I believe in you.
3. You can exceed everyone's expectations of you—especially your own.
4. Life is too short to live constantly stressed. I see how hard

you've worked, and that work ethic means more to me than your grade. It will take you so far in life.

5. You are a gift. Know your worth, and never settle for a bad relationship.

6. I love you, and nothing you do or tell me can make you lose my love.

7. Thank you for making good choices. I know it's not easy.

8. Be a leader.

9. Be a light.

10. Be kind.

11. You have the best heart. I wish I were more like you.

12. You're not meant to carry the weight of the world. That is God's job, so give your worries to Him and pray for guidance.

13. At the end of the day, what matters most is having peace with God and yourself.

14. Seek to bless people, not impress people.

15. I'm so thankful God chose me as your mom. I'd take a hundred kids like you.

16. Don't ever give up on yourself or God. He has a great plan for your life.

17. If you make one bad choice, don't make a second bad choice. Change direction and do the right thing.

18. Get comfortable with being uncomfortable. It's okay to be the only person in the room not doing something. It's okay to leave a party that's getting too wild or to stand alone in a certain decision.

19. There are times in life when you observe, not participate. If people start to do things you don't agree with, leave.

20. This is what some of your classmates are doing, but this is not who you are or who you're meant to be.

21. Decisions are never the same after you drink or do drugs. That's when bad stuff happens and when people can take

advantage of you. You only get one body in life, so be good to it, stay in control, and make healthy choices.

22. You are enough. You have nothing to prove.

23. You may lose more often than you win in life, but that's what makes winning so special.

24. I'm super impressed by the way you've handled this trial. You've shown maturity and grace.

25. Your direction matters more than your speed. Keep doing what you're doing and be patient, because you're on the right track.

26. My life is an open book, and if I can share anything that might help you, I will. I want you to learn from my mistakes.

27. You are too smart not to recognize these bad choices you're making. I'm very upset and disappointed, but I still love you. I'll walk with you as you face the consequences.

28. You always have a choice. Don't let your friends or classmates make choices for you.

29. This mistake is part of your story, not the end of your story. Right your wrong, ask God to forgive you, and move on.

30. How did you feel after making that choice? What would you do differently next time?

31. What will your recovery be? How will you respond to this disappointment or heartache?

32. I get it. (I get that you're stressed/jealous/tired/disappointed because I get stressed/jealous/tired/disappointed as well.) What can I do to help you?

33. Choose wisely who to listen to. Not everyone deserves a voice in your life.

34. I'm so proud of you—not because of your accomplishments but because of who you are.

35. Your family's love for you is bigger than any mistake you can make. We'll always be here for you.

Kindness is essential for the truth to be accepted. As we speak the truth in love, God's Spirit works through us, helping us build a connection even in hard conversations.

Simon Peter answered him, "Lord, to whom shall we go? You have the words of eternal life."

–JOHN 6:68

FIND A SAFE PLACE TO VENT

I know a mom whose daughter is a star athlete. In high school she was captain of her team. Her younger teammates looked up to her, and everyone respected her. She kept their respect by following her mom's advice.

"Stay positive around your teammates," her mom said. "Don't complain, vent, or talk about anyone. Save it for me. Vent to me, and give your best to your team. Encourage them and be a role model."

This advice can apply to parenting as well. Too often we vent to anyone who will listen. We vent on social media—or to total strangers. We unleash on our kids or tell our teenagers that they are self-centered, spoiled, or bratty.

As we do this, we lose respect. We dampen our credibility and weaken our relationships.

I understand a parent's breaking point, yet I'm most sympathetic to the damage our outbursts can cause. Teenagers may look tough externally, but internally they are tender, and they long for the approval of their parents.

In *The 5 Love Languages of Teenagers*, Dr. Gary Chapman says there is a better way to motivate teenagers than by yelling cruel, bitter, or condemning words when they misbehave. He writes:

> Most teenagers are struggling with self-identity. They are comparing themselves with their peers physically, intellectually, and socially. Many are concluding that they simply do not "measure up." Many feel insecure, have little self-esteem, and blame themselves. If there is a stage of life where humans need more affirming words, it would certainly be during the teenage years. Yet this is the very stage at which parents often turn to negative words in their efforts to get the teenager to do what parents believe is best.[6]

Teenagers thrive on words of affirmation, yet mothers also need room to vent, and that is why it helps to have someone— your spouse, your friend, your therapist—who listens well and won't betray your confidence. Having a steel vault who keeps your secrets safe helps you stay strong, especially in front of your kids.

Having a safe outlet also reduces the chance of you dropping a bomb in the heat of the moment. It keeps you under control. Most importantly, it gives you an ally to laugh with as you admit what you *wanted* to say to your daughter versus what you actually said.

Parenting a teenager can test anyone's patience, especially when they get under your skin. It can evoke comments and reactions we later regret. We all mess up, so when you slip, circle back around. Repair the damage quickly. Aim for reconciliation by saying, "I'm so sorry—will you forgive me?" and make a note for next time.

Fighting for your relationship with your daughter is good; fighting with your daughter is not good. There is a difference, and we need God's help to see it. Even in times of tension, you and your daughter are on the same team, serving the same Lord and in need of the same encouragement to think, act, and speak like Him.

———————— • ————————

My dear children, let's not just talk about love; let's practice real love. This is the only way we'll know we're living truly, living in God's reality. It's also the way to shut down debilitating self-criticism, even when there is something to it. For God is greater than our worried hearts and knows more about us than we do ourselves.

–1 JOHN 3:18–20 The Message

———————— • ————————

REFLECTION QUESTIONS

1. Describe a critical remark that an influential person in your life said to you. How did it affect your confidence and self-image?

2. How is blunt criticism different from constructive criticism? Have you ever made a remark to your daughter that you wanted to take back? What did you learn?

3. Have ever you received a correction that went down easy because the person spoke the truth in love? Explain.

4. Have you ever received a piece of advice or criticism at the wrong time? How did poor timing impact your ability to receive the feedback?

5. What is your favorite encouraging phrase to tell your daughter?

6. Who lets you vent and keeps your secrets safe? How can you be a safe place for other moms, not judging them or their teens when they need to talk unfiltered?

. . . .

2

LISTEN AND EMPATHIZE WITH HER WORLD

Most people do not listen with the intent to understand; they listen with the intent to reply.
—DR. STEPHEN R. COVEY[1]

The class bell rang, and suddenly I was walking down the hallway with hundreds of middle schoolers. I'd come to visit a teacher, yet I got caught in this tsunami of students pouring into the main corridor from every direction.

It was mayhem as hundreds of kids hurried to make their next class on time. Some were yelling and goofing off; some whispered with friends; some huddled at lockers. All the stimuli and activity gave me heart palpitations, and I found myself feeling like an insecure, self-conscious middle schooler who simply wanted to blend in with the lockers.

These kids experience this every day, I thought. *They're constantly surrounded by peers who are quick to pounce, judge, or push them out of their way. No wonder it's all about survival, self-preservation, and keeping up their guard to act tougher than they feel. Middle school is a war zone.*

I wondered how I'd feel being surrounded by my peers every day. Would I enjoy being crammed into hallways with hundreds of moms? No way. With all my peers in one place, would I compare myself constantly? Yes. Would my confidence be tested? Of course. Would I be scared to stand out in the wrong way? Definitely.

As an adult, I can choose who to spend time with. If there's a mom I don't trust or have much in common with, I don't have to see her daily. We aren't stuck in classes together or crushing on the same guy. This luxury makes me forget how exhausting it can be to live in a pressure cooker, to be locked into closeness with an array of people and forced into situations that can bring out the best and worst in anyone.

My middle school hallway experience reminded me that my daughters' daily world is very different from my world. Any advice I give them may soon be forgotten as the pressure cooker heats up. Yes, it's hard to parent a teen girl, but I believe it's harder to *be* a teen girl. If we listen and learn about the challenges they face, we can grow a heart for their struggles and relate with more empathy.

We do not have a high priest who is unable to empathize with our weaknesses, but we have one who has been tempted in every way, just as we are—yet he did not sin.

–HEBREWS 4:15

REALITIES OF YOUR DAUGHTER'S WORLD

A girl who made great choices in high school went to college and messed up.

By Christmas break, she was filled with regret. She'd compromised her values, and as she broke down to her high school mentor, crying and beating herself up, her mentor comforted her with truth about God's love and mercy.

"I hate how this is the culture you're dealing with," the mentor said. "It breaks my heart for you and other girls."

This mentor empathized by putting herself in the girl's shoes and acknowledging the lack of virtue in a fallen world. She knew the last thing this girl needed was a lecture because she already felt ashamed. Most importantly, the mentor showed grace. She handled this vulnerable confession with compassion and tenderness.

Because of her loving response, this girl will come back to her for advice, comfort, and support. This mentor will always hold a sacred place in her heart.

As moms, we want vulnerable conversations with our daughters. But how do we take off our mom hats and listen like mentors, being slow to react and not overreacting when we hear something disheartening? Mothers have responsibilities that mentors don't—a call to teach, discipline, protect, correct, guide, and set parameters—and learning to juggle both roles takes time and intention.

I've heard it said that parents play three roles while raising children: cop, coach, and consultant. While a five-year-old needs a cop, a thirteen-year-old needs a coach, and an eighteen-year-old needs a consultant. When our girls are in their teen years, we slowly step back to give them more freedom, intervening when necessary while easing into the role that carries into adulthood.

To be coaches and consultants, we need to understand the teen scene. What cultural trends are shaping them? How can we help them stay centered? What keeps them from living their best lives possible?

Following are some issues we should stay mindful of when considering the realities of our daughters' world.

Fourteen Realities Impacting Today's Teen Girls

1. Anxiety

Anxiety, not depression, is now the leading mental health issue among American youth, and it continues to rise.[2]

Among girls, anxiety has spiked, with research showing the number of girls who often feel nervous, worried, or fearful increasing by 55 percent from 2009 to 2014 (the comparable number for adolescent boys has remained unchanged).[3]

Common causes of anxiety are academic, social, and parental pressures; technology and social media; bullying; perfectionism; fear of failure; overparenting; stress at home; sleep deprivation; unrealistic expectations; and a lack of coping skills.

While some stress is normal and can help your daughter rise to a challenge or recognize a real threat, stress that gets blown out of proportion or stops making sense can turn into anxiety. Girls with anxiety may feel excessive worry, fear, irritability, or restlessness. They may have physical symptoms like nausea, insomnia, heart palpitations, and trouble breathing or concentrating.

Even if your daughter isn't struggling now, anxiety is so prevalent around her that she may struggle one day. Get ahead of any potential pain by staying on top of this conversation. Treat her mental health like her physical health—even having her check in periodically with a mental health counselor like she would a pediatrician.

Being proactive is an emerging response to the mental health epidemic facing today's teens. Even famed University of Alabama Coach Nick Saban, known for his team's domination on a football field, has put the mental well-being of his student-athletes at the top of his agenda.[4] Other schools are following his lead, and I believe this mindset will eventually become mainstream.

Currently, you are your daughter's mental health gatekeeper. You help her prioritize what is and isn't worth the stress. Teach her coping skills, talk about resiliency, give her tools to help her calm down (for example, prayer, exercise, and meditation), and seek a counselor's help when necessary. A counselor can teach your daughter how to face anxiety and talk herself through it in healthy, productive ways.

2. Loneliness, depression, and suicide

According to a Cigna study, young people today are far more likely than senior citizens to report being lonely and in poor health.[5]

God wired all of us to live in community, yet with online interactions replacing face-to-face contact, many teenagers feel isolated, disconnected, and alone. Having two thousand online "friends" means nothing when they have nobody to call with a problem. Seeing every event that they're not invited to can make them question their friends or wonder if they have friends at all.

Since 2012, when the number of Americans who owned smartphones surpassed 50 percent, rates of teen depression and suicide have skyrocketed.[6] For teen girls, the suicide rate is the highest it's been in forty years[7], and depression rates are far higher than those of boys. It's often said that iGen (kids born between 1995 and 2012 and shaped by the cell phone and the rise of social media) is on the brink of the worst mental health crisis in decades. This mental health deterioration can largely be traced back to their phones. As psychologist Dr. Jean Twenge notes, "The more time teens spend looking at screens, the more likely they are to report symptoms of depression."[8]

If you suspect a problem with your daughter, seek help immediately. Even a few sessions with a counselor can protect her mental health and possibly save her life. If you don't see any warning signs, you can assess your daughter's dependence on her phone by how she acts and feels when she's away from it.

3. Social media

Through social media, girls connect after school hours and expand their social networks. They can encourage, inspire, or humor each other no matter where they are.

What nobody anticipated at the birth of social media, however, were the potential downsides of its use. In every community, girls get their feelings hurt, build identities on "likes" and followers, receive hurtful feedback, get caught up in comparisons, develop digital addictions, and have emotional breakdowns due to what they see and absorb.

Social media can mess with your daughter's mind, emotions, and confidence. It can build her up and break her down in a single post.

Relationships need intimacy, and while social media can foster relationships, it can't deepen the roots. The most life-changing moments always happen in person, yet when girls spend too much time online or give social media too much power in their lives, they miss opportunities to experience genuine love.

Make sure your daughter is emotionally ready for popular apps like Instagram, and empower her in advance to handle the ups and downs. Share examples of how you cope when a post in your news feed catches your heart off guard, and teach her to constantly evaluate whether social media is worth her time and attention.

Social media should be fun, and when it stops being fun or

when it causes more feelings of stress, anxiety, jealousy, inade-
quacy, or insecurity than positive connection, it's time to get off
and focus on real-life connections.

4. Too much stimulation, too little downtime

The Internet brings a wide range of stimulation into a person's
private environment, which exposes today's teens to dozens of
stimulations daily, far more than previous generations.[9]

Neuroscientist Dr. Frances Jensen explains, "Every ring,
ping, beep, and burst of song from a smartphone results in an
'Oh, wow' moment in the brain. When the new text message
or post is opened, the discovery is like a digital gift; it releases
a pleasurable rush of dopamine in the brain. In fact, there is
mounting evidence that Internet addiction has much in common
with substance addiction."[10]

With constant connectivity, many teens never decompress.
They miss the downtime they need to rest, relax, and reflect. I
often hear of girls who feel relieved at summer camp without the
stress of their phones. Taking a break helps them see how much
happier they are without the compulsive need to check technology.

Life works best with rhythms, and just as there are times
for your daughter to use technology, there are times to unplug.
Creating space for her soul to breathe and her mind to wander
will help her feel more creative, refreshed, and clear-minded. It
will bring peace and may lead to new ideas or hobbies that come
in those quiet moments away from a noisy world.

5. Labels and an unforgiving society

No matter what choices your daughter makes, she'll get labeled
and teased. If she makes good choices, she may be called a baby,
a perfectionist, or a goody-goody. She'll get excluded from certain
parties. If she makes poor choices, she'll get a reputation. She'll

be called a slut or other names. Either way, people will categorize her and make assumptions based on the stories they hear.

While God is merciful, forgiving anyone with a truly contrite heart, our world is unforgiving, especially to girls. Since today's teens live in a virtual fishbowl, it is important for girls to love each other through their mistakes. It is also important for mothers to help their daughters stand strong in their God-given identities.

Any label that your daughter gets is an *opinion*. What God says about her is a *fact*. Only God can define her, and as she embraces His love for her, she will learn to be confident in who she is, no matter what anyone else says or believes.

6. Bullying and cyberbullying

Bullying used to occur only in person, but through technology, teens can now be bullied at home. Peers can cause damage quickly by spreading a rumor or a picture, and since teenagers don't always have the skills to cope with it, contain it, or set the record straight, it can lead to a downward spiral.

Bullying gets fueled by the lack of empathy in our me-centered society. According to child psychology expert Dr. Michele Borba, teens today are 40 percent less empathetic than just a generation ago, and narcissism is up 58 percent.[11] When teenagers don't feel the pain they inflict on others—or see the hurt reaction on a classmate's face—they may attack them without guilt or remorse. They may type out words they'd never say to someone's face.

There are no easy answers to bullying, and no teenager is safe. Your best defense is to trust God as your daughter's protector and ask Him to cultivate an internal armor that empowers her against hurtful people. Internal strength can help her bounce back if she does get targeted. It can fuel healthy responses and a sense of control as she repurposes her pain, letting God use for good what her peers meant for harm.

7. A culture of secrecy

Technology also gives teenagers a place to test-drive identities and lead multiple lives. From posts that disappear to secret apps to multiple Instagram accounts, teenagers can go underground, creating bold online personas that adults know nothing about.

Your daughter was made to live in the light, yet the world shaping her invites her into the shadows. It packages deceit with bells and whistles and sells it as the latest app.

Explain to your daughter why a culture of secrecy goes against God's will. What seems "normal" in her world is often a slow drift away from God that ultimately leads to pain or shame. Honest living may not seem as exciting as living on the edge, but it will keep her conscience clear and help her sleep well at night.

8. Sleep deprivation

Most teenagers are sleep deprived. They're kept awake by home-work, the blue light emitted from digital screens and TVs that depresses melatonin production, and a body clock that makes them night owls.

Psychologist Dr. Madeline Levine says,

> More than anything, puberty itself drives a change in sleep patterns. Melatonin, which regulates our sleep-wake cycle, is secreted later and later in the evening in these youngsters. As a result, most teens don't feel tired until late at night, usually around midnight. They aren't being difficult or oppositional when they say they can't sleep at ten o'clock. They really can't. This change is called a delayed phase preference and since we can't change biology, we need to optimize their sleeping environment and minimize their biological tendency toward being night owls.[12]

Some school systems set later start times to accommodate teens' body clocks and, as a result, have seen better grades and attendance. Since most schools start at eight, you can help your daughter by separating her from technology before bed and establishing routines—like dimming the lights—that tell her body to wind down.

9. More access to risky behavior

Teenagers have always been drawn to risky behavior, but through the Internet, media, and traveling, they now have more access to it.

Neuroscientist Dr. Frances Jensen explains:

> In centuries past most teens were neatly tucked away on farms. Their range of movement and access to information were limited. And the environments in which they did roam were usually overseen or controlled by adults—parents, teachers, and other authority figures. That meant the potential for bad consequences of risky acts was also limited. It's important for us as parents to remember that just as there are many more bad choices available for teens today, there are many more good ones as well, and we should encourage positive information and experiences for our children.[13]

Dr. Jensen points out how teens are vulnerable to the power of suggestion, and through the computer, they receive many more suggestions than teens did in the past. With substances of abuse more readily available, it only takes a text to access a source of illicit drugs.[14] Besides staying vigilant, you can help your daughter by taking Dr. Jensen's advice to encourage positive experiences and productive uses of her time.

10. Pornography, sexting, promiscuity, and a hook-up culture

When my friend's daughter was in second grade, she hopped out of the pool in her bikini and strutted down the concrete. When her mom asked what she was doing, she said, "I'm shaking my moneymaker."

Her dance studio had taught her the term and the strut, which illustrates how early our society sexualizes girls.

I worry about today's girls and their relationships with boys. I worry about the future of marriage and the lack of real love and respect. Many girls aren't setting standards for themselves, and neither are guys, and from this perfect storm has emerged a hook-up culture that is twisted and wrong.

Girls who don't join the sexting, promiscuous, and hook-up-with-whomever party often think something is wrong with them because they see who gets dates. Girls who do join the party often end up in a counselor's office with emotional scars, regret, and a belief that they're damaged goods and don't deserve a guy who treats them well. Some researchers now compare the level of sexual activity on college campuses to the sexual activity in brothels.[15] Part of the problem is the "anything goes" culture that tells girls there are no moral absolutes and no moral codes to live by.

People assume that pornography is a male-only addiction, but females can get hooked too. Among both genders, a pornography epidemic is on the rise, with most people unaware of the harmful side effects, such as loneliness, depression, anxiety, and trouble building healthy relationships.

Your daughter is in a constant battle to fight the societal forces that sexualize girls, cheapen sex, and distort reality. Help her build a spiritual anchor and a spiritual armor to keep her strong.

11. Disposable friendships

Pope Francis said we live in a throwaway culture where everything is disposable, even relationships, and narcissism makes people incapable of looking beyond themselves. We're quick to connect, disconnect, and block, and we all experience friendships with people who use us for their own benefit.[16] For teenage girls, who tend to make friends their North Star, this causes tremendous heartache and stress.

There is little loyalty in friendships today. Friends often dump each other on a whim and seek new friends when troubles arise instead of working through conflict. In a season of life when girls desperately need friends, they struggle to know which friendships are real and worth fighting for. They see how fake and gossipy some girls can be—calling someone their BFF on Instagram, then dissing her behind her back—and wonder if it's possible to find real friends.

Real friends do exist, but finding them can take time. In chapter 6, you'll find guidance to help your daughter build a support system she can count on.

12. Academic pressures

Most teenagers are stressed by school. It starts early, in sixth or seventh grade, when they're asked to decide what diploma they want to graduate with and what academic track they'd like to be on.

High school gets intense as teenagers prepare for college and competitive admissions. College gets intense as teenagers prepare for real life. We tell girls they have nothing to prove, but frankly, not being a superstar can close doors. Even some sororities will drop rushees with less than a 4.0 GPA. For girls who have less tangible gifts—they can rock a relationship, yet they struggle with math—academics can cause a lot of perceived failure.

Assure your daughter that there are many paths to success.

There are multiple forms of intelligence, and only a few get measured in school. Many teens today will end up in jobs that haven't even been invented yet, and while schools expect students to excel in every subject, in real life, people specialize in jobs that match their strengths.

A high IQ and GPA are certainly assets, but they are not crystal balls into the future. As Stanford University psychology professor Dr. Carol Dweck says in her bestselling book *Mindset*, "A person's true potential is unknown (and unknowable); it's impossible to foresee what can be accomplished with years of passion, toil, and training."[17] This gives hope to all teenagers.

13. Binge drinking and addiction

Today's teenagers are binge drinking, and *what* they're binge drinking can be deadly. For many, vodka and other liquors are the drinks of choice—a far cry from the beer and wine coolers their parents' generation drank to get buzzed.

Whether they drink to fit in, numb emotional pain, blow off steam, or satisfy a curiosity, teens put themselves at risk and possibly set the stage for a lifelong addiction.

"Addiction is more strongly 'hardwired' into the adolescent brain," says neuroscientist Dr. Jensen, "and as rehabilitation centers well know, detox is much harder and fails more often in adolescents, too. Indeed, statistics show that the under-twenty-five population is the fastest-growing age group at inpatient rehab centers."[18]

Adolescents are so primed to learn that it makes them exceedingly vulnerable to learning the wrong things. As Dr. Jensen explains:

> It all goes back to the brain's craving for rewards, and the fact that anything that is learned, good or bad, that stimulates the

production of dopamine is construed by the brain as a reward. This means a little bit of stimulation to a teenage brain whose synapses are firing all over the place leads to a craving for more stimulation that can, in certain situations, result in a kind of overlearning. The more commonly known name for this overlearning is addiction.[19]

Add to this the opioid crisis facing our communities and reaching even our teenagers today, and it becomes highly likely that your daughter will know and love someone who ends up with a serious drug or alcohol problem. There is too much at stake to turn a blind eye, so keep a pulse on your daughter's life and pay attention to red flags.

14. Emptiness

I recently heard of an Ivy League president who said the top struggle he sees on campus is students living with emptiness. Today's teens are highly accomplished yet internally many feel empty. They try to fill their God-shaped hole with friends, parties, love interests, money, achievements, success, vacations, cars, luxuries, and other idols that never satisfy them for long.

Remind your daughter that God planted eternity in her heart. The emptiness she sometimes feels, which earthly pleasures can't gratify, is a longing to be with Him. It's a good desire that will feel complete one day as she enjoys eternity with her Creator. As C. S. Lewis said, "If I find in myself a desire which no experience in this world can satisfy, the most probable explanation is that I was made for another world."[20]

In summary, today's teenage girls face adult-sized realities. They feel tremendous pressure to achieve and chase goals at the expense of their soul. The world that is shaping them is more complex than the world that shaped us, and for every advantage they enjoy, there are heartaches that go with it.

Teenage girls need adults who will listen and try to understand their culture. By hearing them out, we gain access to their world and become better equipped to support them in their journeys.

———————— • ————————

"I have told you these things, so that in me you may have peace. In this world you will have trouble. But take heart! I have overcome the world."

–JOHN 16:33

———————— • ————————

LISTEN WITH EMPATHY

My daughter told me she wanted to quit dance, but I didn't hear her.

After all, she'd danced for five years. Dance was her passion, and she'd begged me to let her try a competitive team. When she was in fifth grade, I caved, and she had a great run. I was thrilled to know she'd discovered her thing, and, deciding that dance must be her track, I signed her up with a coach who could help her with school tryouts the following year.

Then she dropped the news. When the dance season ended, she wanted to hang up her shoes.

I thought the feeling would pass because my daughters have wanted to quit things before and changed their minds, but four months later she felt the same way. Even a dance intensive with good friends in New York City couldn't entice her to stay with it.

The hardest part for me was the lack of a backup plan; there was nothing else she wanted to try.

I realized then how it unsettled me not to know my daughter's track. Letting go of dance was like letting go of a security blanket that gave me false confidence and might give her a place of belonging as she entered middle school. Even though she had great friends and would eventually find her "thing," I craved security. I had to come to peace with letting her make this choice.

Ironically, my daughter returned to dance eight months later. One day out of the blue, she texted me from a friend's house to announce her desire to try out for the school team because her friends talked her into it. She made the team, found an instructor she loved, and bounced back with renewed motivation. Best of all, I saw her dancing around our house again. Her old joy had been rekindled—yet this never would have happened if I'd pushed the issue and not let her make her own choice.

Too often we don't hear our children because we assume that we're the experts. We listen, yet in the back of our minds, our decisions are set. We're convinced we are right before they even make a case. We have subconscious goals or agendas that cloud our thinking.

Sometimes we think we're looking out for our children, but what really drives our response is how their choices affect (or reflect on) us.

- *She can't go to college in California; that's thirteen hours away from home!*
- *She can't join that team; everyone in our family has always been part of this one.*
- *I've spent five years driving her to every club volleyball tournament in the country. We're too invested to give up. She can push through the burnout and exhaustion.*
- *People will think she's antisocial if she stays home every Friday night. It bothers me how she never wants to go to parties.*

Someone once said, "Most people hear, but few people listen." As parents, our failure to listen is usually due to a preoccupation with our thoughts. Instead of listening to learn, we listen to respond, waiting for a chance to make a point or teach a lesson. In the process, we miss getting to know our child's thoughts, feelings, and dreams.

It is possible to listen and empathize with a teenager even when we disagree. I have learned—from my husband listening and playing therapist to me—that listening calmly and being a sounding board keeps a person talking. It offers a safe place to be heard.

You can relate to your daughter without compromising your values. If she says, "I'm frustrated because I make better choices than my friends, but they have fewer rules," you can reply, "That's a good point, and I understand your frustration. You won't understand every choice we make, but let's talk about it because there may be another area where we can extend more freedom."

This conversation might lead to a later curfew on certain nights. You may find wiggle room in an old rule from two years ago that needs to be updated anyway. By letting your daughter win some minor battles, you help her feel that she has a say in her life and remind her that you're on her side.

Anytime that your daughter opens up to you is a privilege. The opportunity may not come again. Take these moments, even if the timing is not ideal, and listen attentively. Be a voice of reason when it's your turn to talk, sharing your thoughts and wisdom after reflecting on what you heard.

———————— • ————————

To answer before listening—that is folly and shame.
—PROVERBS 18:13

———————— • ————————

HOW DO YOU SEE TEEN GIRLS?

I was in Atlanta for a college football national championship game when I noticed an interesting dynamic.

Our hotel was packed with fans from across the country. Since the rooms weren't ready yet, guests were told to check their bags at the front desk and freshen up in the lobby bathrooms.

In one bathroom was a small group of sorority girls. They were spread across several sinks, applying makeup. One woman exited her stall, shot the girls a dirty look, and asked the custodian for hand sanitizer to avoid joining them at an open sink. Another woman exited her stall and smiled when she saw these girls. She joined them excitedly at the sink, told them how cute they were, and began asking questions.

With laughter and showstopping smiles, these girls came alive. They were so kind to this Midwestern woman who took an interest in their lives, and as they fed off each other's energy, the bathroom gained a positive vibe.

Same girls, opposite women. While one woman assumed the worst, the other saw the best.

There is great negativity toward teenage girls these days. While some of it is understandable, much of it comes from hasty evaluations and preconceived notions: adults seeing only short skirts, self-absorption, or vanity and being quick to judge, condemn, or act holier-than-thou.

To no surprise, girls don't like these adults, and they certainly won't seek or take to heart their advice.

It is worth considering which camp we fall in. As moms, we have concerns that upset us and frustrate us: problems we see, hearts we long to change, issues we're desperate to fix. But in our quest to raise decent and kind human beings, do we stop, listen, and empathize? Do we treat our daughters like sisters in Christ?

Do we take off our parenting hat at times and try to understand their lives?

Our girls were made for more than the culture that is shaping them. And while we can't blame the culture for the choices they make, we can acknowledge what they're up against. We can discuss the struggles of being human. Most of all, we can model God's strength and compassion. We can listen to our girls and then listen to Him, bringing grace and wisdom into our responses.

———————— • ————————

"My command is this: Love each other as I have loved you."

—JOHN 15:12

———————— • ————————

REFLECTION QUESTIONS

. . . .

1. Who listens to you attentively? How can you apply their approach when listening to your daughter?

2. Today's teenagers face bigger challenges than their parents' generation. They're being shaped by a world that is more complex and less forgiving. Do you try to understand their culture, or do you keep a safe distance because knowing too much is stressful?

3. How can empathy promote civil conversations when you and your daughter disagree? Is it easy or hard to put yourself in her shoes?

4. What is your biggest concern about the realities of teen culture? How can you empower your daughter in this area?

5. Describe a time when you listened to your daughter but failed to "hear" her because your mind was consumed with your plans, feelings, or worries. What did you learn?

6. What comes to mind when you see a group of teenage girls? Are you intimidated, annoyed, or curious? Do you jump to stereotypes and conclusions, or do you get to know them before forming an opinion? Explain.

. . . .

3

BE HER MOM

You are preparing for the launching of a young adult into the world. Wise parents keep the imminent catapulting of their teens into society in the back of their minds at all times. The question they must always struggle with is no longer, "How can I make them behave?" but rather, "How can I help them survive on their own?"
–DR. HENRY CLOUD AND DR. JOHN TOWNSEND[1]

My friend Jennifer enjoyed a wonderful upbringing, and throughout her life she remained exceptionally close to her parents. So when her father died at age eighty and her mother passed away three years later, she experienced the heavy loss of suddenly being parentless.

Jennifer was with her daughter, Caroline, a fourth grader

at the time, when the heartbreaking news about her mother came. Immediately Caroline threw her arms around her. They hugged and cried, and after a moment, Caroline looked up at Jennifer with fear in her eyes and said, "Mom, you don't have any parents!"

Jennifer could tell that Caroline was sad for her *and* scared for her. Through a ten-year-old lens, being parentless seemed unimaginable. Quick to reassure her daughter, Jennifer replied, "Caroline, I am devastated to lose my mom and not have parents. But they spent their entire lives preparing me for this day: the day I'd have to stand on my own two feet. They taught me how to handle life without them. That's what I hope Daddy and I are doing for you and Davis, so that one day you won't need us the way you need us now."

Caroline hugged her mom again, still saddened by the loss yet comforted by these words.

Every time I think of Jennifer's story, I want to cry, yet I also believe it epitomizes the goal of good parenting: to teach our children to stand on their own two feet. To equip them to handle life without us. To prepare them for the day when we aren't here anymore and they must take the torch and carry it into the future.

Let's be clear: we never stop needing our parents, not when love exists. I've met ninety-year-old women who still ache for their mothers and wish they were alive. Our parents can teach us everything except how to stop missing them. Even as grown-ups, when we can pay our own bills and shop for our own groceries, we need our parents for encouragement, advice, and friendship. We value their opinions and want to share stories from our lives. Nobody can fill the void that opens in their physical absence.

At the same time, we serve a mighty God. He helps us move

forward while wiping our tears and allowing us to feel the voids that remind us that earth is not our final home. Only in heaven will we feel perfect peace and joy as we meet our Creator and reunite with loved ones.

You and I have limited time on this planet. God has temporarily entrusted our daughters to our care. He wants us to enjoy them and shape them. This means making some hard calls and parenting them with a love that includes boundaries, rules, consequences, discipline, and generous amounts of grace.

What makes our daughters happy as teenagers is different from what will make them happy as mature adults. If we parent them correctly, they won't like us some days. They won't understand every choice we make. But as a priest told me, love wants what is best for a person *long-term*. Love keeps the big picture in mind.

I often think of who I hope my daughters will be at age forty, and I work backward to ask, "What can I do *today* to cultivate those qualities?" I remember these words from youth pastor Cameron Cole: "We aren't parenting for our sixteen-year-old to like us. We're parenting for our forty-year-old to respect us."

A child's opinion of a parent evolves over time. What seems unfair now will (hopefully) make more sense down the road. A man whom I respect greatly told me that the day he graduated from college, his father became the smartest man he knew. Only then, with a mature mindset, could he see the depth of his father's love and understand many past decisions.

More important than pleasing your teenager is pleasing God. He's the One we answer to at the end of our lives. He's the One who evaluates and rewards us based on how well we handle what He entrusts to us.[2] So stay strong, my friend, and let the Holy Spirit work. Ask for the grace to equip your daughter to stand on her own two feet.

---•---

No discipline seems pleasant at the time, but painful. Later on, however, it produces a harvest of righteousness and peace for those who have been trained by it.

—HEBREWS 12:11

---•---

IF YOU DON'T PARENT HER, WHO WILL?

A mother told her teenager's psychologist, "I need you to work on the phone thing with her because she's on it all the time."

The psychologist politely replied that setting phone limits was the mother's job. Ultimately, she holds the key.

We forget this, don't we? In an age of parenting when we can farm out practically anything—enlisting the help of sitters, nannies, tutors, counselors, ACT coaches, college advisers, athletic trainers, dinner delivery services, party planners, even Uber drivers—our initial response to a need is often, "Who can I call for help?"

Sometimes outside expertise is needed, and sometimes time constraints make convenience worth the cost. But there are many parts of parenting we can't afford to outsource. Your daughter has only one mother, and if you don't parent her, who will?

It's hard to be the mom, especially if disciplining falls largely on you. With teenagers, you know what decisions set them off. You can anticipate the pushback when their friends get an app they aren't allowed to have. You dread disrupting the peace.

Parenting gets lonely as your kids grow up and the diversity in parenting styles widens. Parents who once shared your beliefs may start making different choices—and suddenly you're the lone ranger with an unhappy daughter who is angry about your rules.

But remember: the popular thing to do may not be the right

thing for your family. It's okay to have your own rules and support other families with their own rules too.

It's normal for your daughter to separate from you, want independence, and develop an identity apart from your family. Knowing how much rope to give her, however, or how much guidance and protection she still needs is unclear. You don't know for certain how much freedom she is ready for.

Then there's this: the teenage brain isn't like an adult brain. Even the sharpest minds aren't firing on all cylinders. Teenage brains are only 80 percent developed, and to understand the implications, we turn to science and experts like neuroscientist Dr. Frances Jensen, who shares these important insights (and many more) in *The Teenage Brain*:

1. **The teenage brain has limitations** when it comes to controlling impulses, assessing risk, avoiding peer pressure, and understanding the consequences of one's actions.[3]
2. **We, as adults, are legally responsible for our children until they turn eighteen.** We must take the lead and try to think for them until their own brains can take over. Since the most important part of the brain, the frontal lobe (where actions are weighed, situations are judged, and decisions are made), is the last part of the brain to develop, we need to serve as our teens' frontal lobes until their brains are fully wired and ready to go on their own.[4]
3. **Adolescents are impulsive and prone to risk-taking.** They're motivated by novelty and sensation-seeking. An underdeveloped prefrontal cortex means they have trouble seeing ahead and understanding consequences of their actions. This leaves them ill-equipped to judge the harm of risky behavior.[5]
4. **Teenagers are capable of remarkable achievements**, thanks to dynamically changing, growing, and flexible brains. The

downside of this "open" and excitable brain is that it can be adversely affected by stress, drugs, chemical substances, and environmental changes—resulting in dramatically more serious problems than adults would face.[6]

5. **Teenagers may look and think like adults in some ways,** and their ability to learn is staggering, but knowing what their limitations are (cognitively, emotionally, and behaviorally) is critically important.[7]

6. **Teenagers are especially vulnerable to emotional and psychiatric issues.** They are hypersensitive to stress, and their peers may not notice the warning signs or offer adequate empathy. Adults who spend time with teenagers need to stay vigilant, ask good questions, probe, stay connected, and—most importantly—have a low threshold to seek medical advice or counseling for symptoms that appear out of the ordinary. With kids spending so much time isolated online, warning signs may be harder to detect.[8]

7. **Biology makes substances of abuse more irresistible to teenagers than to adults.** Even "good" kids can mingle with the "wrong" kids and easily fall into the trap of substance abuse. Adults and even teen peers should keep a very watchful eye on signs of drug abuse (such as withdrawal, dramatic changes in appetite and sleeping habits, excessive irritability, and lack of personal hygiene). We should have a low threshold for suspicion and aggressively intervene when needed because only with aggressive intervention can teens recover.[9]

8. **As children leave childhood, adults lose physical control.** Our best tool during adolescence is our ability to advise, explain, and be good role models.[10]

In short, teenagers need their parents. They're making big choices with lifelong consequences, and their mistakes can be immortalized on social media. They're great at learning (better than adults) and highly influenced by their environment because they absorb it. Their brains are primed to learn, yet learning the wrong things can escalate quickly into disaster.

Add to this a predisposition toward risky behavior, heavy struggles, and a brain that can't fully regulate impulse control or judgment, and it is clear why teenagers need guidance.

As moms, we can help our daughters learn to think like adults. We can teach them to say no, listen to their conscience, and discern God's will. Ultimately, your daughter's life is her own. She'll make her own decisions and live with her own mistakes. You can't control her, but you can be a voice of reason and set boundaries that protect her.

If your choices and boundaries anger her at times, it's okay. As Sissy Goff reminds us, "Don't be afraid to be the parent. Your teenager's like or dislike of you is more about his or her adolescent angst than it is about your style of parenting. Your teens will come back around as they grow up, and they'll respect you more for being the steady, strong parent God has made you to be."[11]

Showing your daughter what a strong, confident woman looks like helps her become a strong, confident girl. After all, she learns from your example. Too many girls today are scared to think for themselves. They let their friends dictate what they do. They cave to peer pressure and feel no control over their lives. If you desire more for your daughter, let her witness more in your life. Keep God first and aim to do what's right.

———————— • ————————

God has not given us a spirit of fear and timidity, but of power, love, and self-discipline.

–2 TIMOTHY 1:7 NLT

———————— • ————————

PREPARE YOUR CHILD FOR THE ROAD, NOT THE ROAD FOR YOUR CHILD

A group of girls on a Christian retreat were taken to a mountain-top and told to listen to their fathers.

One at a time, they were blindfolded and told what steps to take. Since cliffs were nearby, they had to walk slowly and deliberately.

Each blindfolded girl was told to listen to her dad. Her dad was instructed to speak softer and softer until his voice became a whisper. Meanwhile, the girls watching were told to gradually get louder and louder to drown out the father's voice. After several steps, each blindfolded girl would panic as she asked, "Daddy, where do I go? I can't hear you!" because the noise was too loud. As her peers screamed louder, her father's voice was lost.

I love this exercise and its application to listening to God. For teenagers, who constantly get bombarded by outside voices, tuning in to God's quiet whispers can make a huge difference in where they end up. It can protect them and steer them away from nearby cliffs.

Adolescence is a time of dangerous new territory. To blindly let our daughters loose without any instruction would be irresponsible. Unlike us, they haven't lived long enough to see tragedies. They don't know what can happen from a seemingly harmless choice. They don't believe us when we share stories of potentially fatal outcomes.

We can't always save them, but we can prepare them the best we can for treacherous terrain. Here are critical conversations to get you started.

Twenty Ways to Prepare Your Daughter for the Road

1. Let your daughter know that you're on her side.

As you hear about her peers making poor choices, empathize with your daughter's position. Acknowledge the difficulty of standing strong.

You may say, "I hate this social scene you're dealing with. It's tougher than what I faced. My priorities are your safety and honesty. Be honest, even if you mess up, because I need to know the truth to help you. I love you so much; I'd take a bullet for you. I'd rescue you from the seediest part of town, so don't ever hesitate to call me out of fear of getting in trouble. Even if I'm upset, I'll get over it if you're safe. What I'd never get over is losing you, so please value your life as much as I do."

2. Talk about five-second decisions.

A mom was at the lake with her daughter and her daughter's friends when two sixteen-year-old boys pulled up on a boat and invited the girls to ride. The mom had to quickly decide whether to let them go, and since she wasn't sure about the boys' boating skills or if they'd been drinking (she knew they'd recently been busted), she said no. It wasn't worth the risk.

Parents and teenagers alike face "five-second decisions" that randomly pop up. For your daughter, the decision could involve peer pressure at a party or participating in a prank. Pray in advance for wisdom. Tell your daughter to trust her gut and err on the side of safety. Before she goes to a party, talk about exit strategies, and give her permission to blame you to save face or get out of a bad situation.

3. Talk about choices and consequences.

Every choice has a consequence, and it will take a thousand good choices for your daughter to get where she wants to be. Even small choices, like being kind, impact who she becomes and what friends she attracts.

Allowing your daughter to face the consequences of poor decisions prepares her for reality. Getting detention because she got smart with a teacher may keep her from mouthing off to her boss one day. Taking away her phone because she lied about a text may teach her to be honest. Making her work to pay off a speeding ticket may make her think twice before speeding again.

All her choices matter, but the choices she makes on Friday and Saturday nights (or over summer and spring break) can make or break her. They can ruin her reputation, set a harmful or physically dangerous trajectory, and bond her with the wrong friends.

Your daughter will reap what she sows. Learning early that positive choices create a positive life while negative choices lead to dead-end roads can help prevent future heartaches.

4. Talk about living within the boundaries of "wise freedom."

When your daughter turns sixteen, the concept of free will kicks in. She'll face more choices and situations than ever before.

With freedom comes responsibility, and what spiritually healthy people know is that God gives us rules out of love. His blueprint for living helps us enjoy His best plan for us.

As parents set boundaries, teenagers push boundaries. Letting your daughter suffer real-life consequences as she crosses your limits can teach her unforgettable life lessons. The hope is that one day she'll set her own limits. She'll live within the boundaries of wise freedom due to intrinsic motivation (it makes her feel good and draws her closer to God) rather than extrinsic motivation (she's scared of getting in trouble and wants people to think she's "good").

5. Talk about her conscience and living by a moral code.

Some people make terrible choices yet feel no shame afterward because their conscience is asleep or dead.

Your daughter should know that her conscience is a gift. Without it, she'd never feel guilt or remorse. She'd have no incentive to change, apologize, confess her sins, think twice, or turn back to God.

The authors of *Parenting Teens with Love and Logic* write, "Children who are parented well gradually develop an internal voice that says, 'I wonder how my next decision is going to affect me and those around me?' This voice comes from having made bad decisions and living with the consequences while experiencing the love and empathy of their parents. This voice is far more important than all the external controls parents can think up."[12]

Naturally, we want what's best for our daughters, but do they want the best for themselves? Through a healthy conscience shaped by the Holy Spirit, your daughter can develop a moral code to live by and learn from.

6. Encourage her to set standards, especially with guys.

Your daughter should hear this: "You and every girl you know are better than the lifestyle this world pushes on girls. Set a high bar for yourself and know the best guys will rise to the challenge."

Too often girls get caught up in a promiscuous or permissive lifestyle. They use their sexuality to compete for male attention—and end up feeling used, broken, or damaged.

Meanwhile, the world tells boys that sexual conquest makes them a "man." Especially in the teen years, they get applauded for objectifying girls. This mindset is toxic, yet it is reality, and your daughter needs to be aware. While some boys will question society's message to them, others will buy into it. They'll pursue easy opportunities and take advantage of girls.

Again, your daughter will get teased no matter what choices she makes, so she may as well make choices that she can be proud of. Whatever she chooses, she's still a child of God, loved beyond measure even on her worst day.

7. Talk about joy.

An ACT coach told me, "I tell my students they need two things in life: a job and a hobby. If their hobby becomes their job, they need a new hobby."

I love this viewpoint because it's refreshing. In a world where every activity has a purpose—and career planning begins in childhood—teenagers need hobbies they enjoy for fun. Whether they're gifted or accomplished doesn't matter because the joy they get from painting, singing, acting, dancing, writing, building, playing intramural sports, or pursuing a passion makes their heart sing.

Life is too short to lose joy. More than an inner Picasso, your daughter needs an inner child who reminds her how to play.

8. Set high expectations (and share your stories of failure).

Dr. Carol Dweck says, "Great teachers set high standards for all their students, not just the ones who are already achieving."[13]

Great parents set high expectations, too, and empower their children to meet them. They also create a culture of grace and restoration. As my daughter's history teacher once told his class, we can't give teenagers high expectations and not share stories of failure. Too many teens are scared to fail because the world expects perfection. Since adolescence is a time for your daughter to take healthy risks, face her fears, bounce back, and gain confidence by doing what feels impossible, she needs adults in her life who openly share their stories of failure.

Tell your daughter about a time you failed to be a good friend . . . lost your temper . . . told a lie . . . hurt someone . . . had your heart broken . . . made a poor choice . . . took a shortcut . . . wrongly accused someone . . . humiliated yourself . . . or fell flat on your face. Talk about God's mercy and the transforming grace of Jesus. Our worst failures are our best teachers, so make sure your daughter knows how God can use any experience to impart life-changing lessons.

9. Keep a watchful eye.

It's good for your daughter to know that you'll inspect what you expect. Keeping a watchful eye is a mother's duty, and it keeps her accountable (and mindful) when she knows you'll check in.

Monitoring keeps teenagers safe. You don't want to suffocate your daughter or hover, but you do want to know who she's with, where she's going, who might be there, and what situations she could end up in (often unpredictable, even to her). Keep a pulse on her friendships and trust your instincts, because when something or someone gives you pause, a deeper investigation could save her life.

10. Initiate hard conversations.

You know who enjoys an awkward conversation less than you? Your daughter! That is why you must take the lead—because she won't.

Awkward conversations get easier with practice. I believe in staying ahead of topics and discussing them before they're fully relevant because your daughter will hear and see things sooner than you think.

After my first book for teen girls was released, older parents told me, "You think you can wait until high school to have these conversations, but you can't. It's almost too late. They need this advice in middle school, if not sooner." Due to technology, kids are growing up faster, and parents who think they're protecting their kids by not addressing hard realities often have kids who don't tell them what's really happening.

What keeps me brave is remembering what a youth pastor once told me about "setting the first tracks." Imagine your daughter at the top of a ski slope, facing a perfect blanket of snow. That snow is her young mind: innocent, pure, unblemished. Soon, skiers will come down and set tracks in the snow. Whoever sets the *first* tracks will leave a particularly deep impression that your daughter will never forget.

As parents, we want to set the first tracks. We want to ski down first and impress the truth in our daughters' minds so that when other people ski down and set tracks, our girls know which tracks to trust. Establishing ourselves upfront as the authority helps us become their go-to person. It lets our daughters know they can come to us with questions they'll inevitably take somewhere—if not to us, then to Google or a friend.

Talk to your teenage daughter about sex, pornography, sexual assault, sexuality, nude pictures, sex trafficking, body changes, STDs, the hook-up culture, and other nitty-gritty topics. Give her real-life stories that illustrate how drugs and alcohol set the stage for terrible choices and why it's imperative to keep her radar up. Use news stories as a launching pad for conversations about character, good judgment, and learning from people's mistakes.

Approaching nitty-gritty topics from God's perspective, explaining how we (as sinful humans) take the good things He created and warp them in ways He never intended, helps your daughter understand why we need an ultimate source of truth. Rather than a Google search, what many of your daughter's questions call for is a God search.

11. Talk about self-awareness.

"We think temptation lies around us," pastor Rick Warren says, "but God says it begins *within* us. If you didn't have the internal desire, the temptation could not attract you. Temptation always starts in your mind, not in circumstances."[14]

We all have vulnerabilities and blind spots, so what are your daughter's? What people or situations entice her to cave? What tempts her to do what she swore she wouldn't do?

If she is a people pleaser, she may tell people what they want to hear, even if it means telling white lies. If she craves attention from boys, she may manipulate them or be easily manipulated. If she is introverted or meek, she may cower against strong personalities. If she hates to disappoint a friend, she may say yes when she wants to say no and secretly grow resentful.

Sharing stories from your life will help your daughter examine her life.

You may admit how you used to be bossy, and it kept you from making friends until you realized how off-putting your bossiness could be.

You may tell her about the weekend you spent with some gossipy moms, how you gossiped like crazy to fit in, and only as you drove home did you feel sick to your stomach. You realized then the need to avoid this group in the future because it brought out the worst in you.

You may even tell your daughter about the time in high school when you snuck alcohol into a school trip to be cool. You shared it with some freshmen boys, and years later, when you heard one of those freshmen became an alcoholic, you felt guilty and wondered if you played a role. It weighed on you for years, until you worked up the nerve to call him and apologize.

How openly you share with your daughter is a personal call. Share small examples and go from there, knowing that any real-life stories you offer drive the lesson home.

12. Remind her to get comfortable with being uncomfortable.

It's important for your daughter to know she always has a choice. Even if her best friends do something she doesn't agree with, she can leave or stand alone.

A moment of pleasure isn't worth a lifetime of regret. In every season, your daughter will face situations that make her uncomfortable, and by learning to push through them, she gains a valuable life skill.

13. Empower her to say no.

What starts many girls down the wrong path is the inability to say no. Pediatrician Dr. Meg Meeker says this:

Parents often tell me, "My daughter is a really good kid. She knows right from wrong and that drinking is trouble. If she were at a party, I have no doubt she would do the right thing."

But I see really good kids all the time who got in trouble because they didn't know how to say no, because their parents hadn't prepared them for the situations in which they found themselves, because their parents expected a teenager to make a decision that an adult should have made. Even the best of daughters want to please their friends. You must assume that whatever her friends do, she'll do.

Finally, remember, nice girls die in car accidents. Nice girls get pregnant. Nice girls fall for bad boys. Teaching your daughter to say no could save her life.[15]

In the book *Boundaries*, the authors declare *no* to be the most basic boundary-setting word. It tells people that you exist apart from them, and you are in control of you.[16] The authors explain how boundaries are a "litmus test" for the quality of a relationship because people who can respect your boundaries will love your will, your opinions, and your separateness, while those who can't respect your boundaries will only love your compliance—your *yes* but not your *no*.[17]

Teaching your daughter to say no safeguards her mind, heart, body, and soul. It allows her to be a good steward of the gifts that God gave her.

14. Talk about mental health.

Sadly, today's teenagers are the first generation of teenagers to feel more stressed than their parents, except during the summer months.[18]

While this isn't surprising, it is troubling. We can't let the world (or its expectations) steal the joy of adolescence and the exuberance of youth.

More than anyone, you know your daughter's strengths and limitations. You understand her daily obstacles. Maybe she has a learning disability and struggles to get Bs. Maybe she gets recommended for every advanced class, but she stays up until 2:00 a.m. to get her schoolwork done. Maybe she plays a competitive sport, and when she gets home at 9:00 p.m., she still has four hours of homework. Maybe she shuts down in a big or loud environment.

Train your daughter to protect her mental health. Talk about balance, self-awareness, and making choices that reflect her goals. What's right for her friend may not be right for her, and if she feels consumed by stress—exhausted, depleted, withdrawn, isolated from friends and a normal teenage life—it's time for a change. Nobody can live with their foot to the pedal, and scaling back to a manageable load can prevent burnout and even a crash.

Half of all mental illnesses start in adolescence, so teach your daughter now to pay attention to red flags, know what helps her thrive, and seek help when needed.

15. Talk about self-image, self-love, and being kind to her body.

For teen girls today, Instagram is a second mirror. Even girls with a healthy self-image may see themselves in a new light as they compare their bodies to the perfect bodies in their news feed—or as they suddenly feel big next to their skinny friends in pictures.

Your daughter gets bombarded with unrealistic images and ideals. Even if you say the right things at home, she'll hear the wrong messages from the world. Our society worships perfection, and the prettier and skinnier a girl gets, the more praise and attention she receives. What logically follows is a quest for perfection that keeps many girls seeking applause in areas dangerous to their health.

How can you help? By discussing healthy self-love. Reminding your daughter that God created her with *intention* and *attention*, and nothing about her is a mistake. Your daughter only gets one body in life, and it must last her a long time, so encourage her to take care of it. Help her build healthy habits with food, exercise, and lifestyle choices that she'll carry into adulthood.

Like many girl moms, I worry about eating disorders (95 percent of people with eating disorders are between the ages of twelve and twenty-five[19]), and I talk to my girls about the warning signs of heading in that direction.

Most moms have heard of anorexia, bulimia, and binge eating, but be aware of a new eating disorder called orthorexia, which has evolved with the clean food movement. What begins as an effort to eat healthy can send girls down a slippery slope where they slowly cut out entire food groups and develop an unhealthy obsession with eating only "pure" foods. They eliminate processed foods, then meat, then dairy, then carbs, and so on until they get down to ten or fewer foods that they allow themselves to eat. Unlike other eating disorders, orthorexia is rooted in a need to be "healthy" rather than a preoccupation with appearance or losing weight, but the physical consequences are the same: life-threatening.

Good things become bad things when taken to extremes. Make this part of your conversation as you talk to your daughter about moderation and balance.

16. Talk about being assertive and speaking up for her needs.

Every girl's voice deserves to be heard, and every girl needs guidance with using her voice wisely.

Some girls have a strong voice and say exactly what they think—yet they lack tact and warmth. They hurt people's feelings because they have no filter.

Other girls have a kind voice. They're loved and respected—but they don't speak up. They let people take advantage of them and feel powerless over their lives.

It is possible to be strong *and* kind. Honest *and* tactful. Assertive *and* congenial.

More than ever, our daughters need healthy assertion. In a society where people will walk all over other people—and prey on the weak—girls should know how to take up for themselves, tell a friend when that friend has hurt their feelings, and let boys down.

The tenth-grade girl who never learns to say, "I love our friendship, but you can't treat me like that" may find her friends gradually treating her worse. She may get stuck in a negative loop until she stands up for herself.

The eighth-grade girl who never learns to tell a friend she hurt her feelings may see her hurt leak out through passive-aggressive behavior or talking about her friend behind her back. She may miss the chance to work through conflict and deepen her friendships.

And the sixth-grade girl who agrees to "go" with a boy she doesn't like because she's scared to hurt his feelings may be easily pressured later with this people-pleasing mentality.

If your daughter is naturally strong, she may need help with being less abrasive and more sensitive to the needs of others. If your daughter is naturally sensitive—and wants others to be happy—she may need assurance that her needs and desires matter too. As she speaks up in small ways, voicing an opinion of where to eat dinner or what to name the new puppy, and has those requests met, she'll build the confidence to speak up in bigger ways too.

17. Model appropriate alcohol use.

My friend stopped drinking alcohol because she noticed how she gossiped more when she had too much. As her kids became teenagers, however, she wanted them to see what drinking in moderation looks like. So if a family came over for dinner, or if they had friends to the lake, she drank a glass or two of wine to model a mature approach.

Sadly, binge drinking is largely what teenagers see, among peers and sometimes parents. Many teenagers give no thought to the legal implications, the risks, their tolerance, or what they've eaten that day. They lose control of their bodies and their ability to keep themselves safe. They make decisions they'd never make sober—like riding with a drunk driver or hooking up with a friend's date—and often don't even remember.

Talk to your daughter about alcohol—both the wise use and misuse. Explain why the legal age is twenty-one, and why drinking alcohol legally and responsibly keeps it enjoyable. Discuss alcoholism, especially if there are alcoholics in your family, and how it evolves slowly over time. Make sure your daughter understands that the more committed she is to taking care of herself, the better choices she can make.

18. Talk about addiction.

A seasoned member of Alcoholics Anonymous told me the newcomers are getting younger and younger. Sadly, we have a culture where ninth graders need rehab and become part of a club that nobody wants to be in.

If you know an addict—or have seen/experienced what an addict's decisions can cost them—you wouldn't wish addiction on anyone. And when you hear about middle schoolers drinking or college coeds doing drugs, it logically follows that many of today's casual users will end up battling lifelong problems.

Here are sobering facts to share with your daughter:

- "A person stops maturing at the age that they start abusing substances."[20]
- "Of the 10.5 million youths who had taken a drink, nearly 7 million admitted to binge drinking, and more than 40 percent of individuals who start drinking before the age of thirteen will develop alcohol abuse problems later in life, according to a report in the *Journal of Substance Abuse*."[21]
- "The pot teens smoke today is up to *seven* times more

potent than what was available twenty or more years ago."[22]

- "With a still-maturing brain, teens are especially vulnerable to drugs that work directly on the brain's chemistry. . . . Nine out of ten addicts say they first used drugs before they were eighteen years old."[23]

Addiction affects the rich and the poor, and since genetics plays a role, nobody knows which child in a family might be pre-disposed. Even a healthy adult is not "safe" from addiction, and since all of us are susceptible to this slippery slope, it's important to be compassionate and help those who struggle.

19. Talk about discernment and spiritual warfare.

A college freshman told her mother that she'd found her dream sorority. The girls were friendly, happy, and fun.

Her mother told her to pray that she'd end up where God wanted her to be, not where her flesh wanted to be. Her daughter thought these girls were her people until they invited her out one night and stopped by an apartment—where she saw five girls from this sorority snorting cocaine.

She was shocked, yet thankful, that her eyes were opened before she pledged.

We all get blindsided, don't we? Sometimes trouble is clear, and sometimes it hides behind pretty faces. Sometimes trouble develops slowly in front of us, and we don't recognize it for what it is.

In Matthew 10:16, Jesus said, "I am sending you out like sheep among wolves. Therefore be as shrewd as snakes and as innocent as doves." The enemy is often subtle in deceiving us. He wants to divert, distract, disarm, and trip us up to separate us from God. We need divine intervention to be kind *and* smart. Gentle *and* shrewd. Soft *and* strong. Brave *and* quick to escape danger.

Your daughter is entering a world of unpredictable situations, so pray for discernment and trustworthy friends. Remind her to look beyond what's shiny or impressive and trust her instincts. When something doesn't feel right, it's usually not right, and when she suddenly discovers that she was blindsided, she can thank God for the lesson.

20. Talk about healthy relationships.

I've heard it said, "You marry to your level of health." This is true in friendships as well.

Healthy people attract healthy friends. Unhealthy people attract unhealthy friends. If your daughter wants healthy relationships, she must get herself in a good place mentally, emotionally, physically, and spiritually.

This may mean letting a friend go—or accepting that her friend let her go. It may mean going to church alone, seeking help from a counselor, doing volunteer work, or avoiding situations that bring her guard down.

Equipping your daughter for the road ahead is no small feat. Empower her to feel prepared, not scared, and help her tune in to her Father's voice, trusting Him for direction with every step she takes.

They do not fear bad news; they confidently trust the LORD to care for them.

–PSALM 112:7 NLT

RULES AND RELATIONSHIP

Some parents build relationships with their children. Some parents set rules. Wise parents do *both*.

The question is, where do we draw the lines? How do we balance the two so we're not pushovers or dictators? We all know adults who don't talk to their parents because they were insanely strict. We also know adults whose lives became train wrecks because nobody put on the brakes.

Both extremes are unhealthy, and as the authors of *Boundaries* note, "The too-strict parent runs the risk of alienating the almost adult from the home connection. The too-lenient parent wants to be the child's best friend at a time the teen needs someone to respect."[24]

Many parents opt to be their teenager's friend to keep open communication. Their permissiveness keeps their teen talking and deters sneaky behavior. Today's trend of "buddy parenting" is largely a response to the authoritarian parenting our generation grew up with. While our parents had more control, there wasn't always a strong emotional connection, and today's parents desire more connection and closeness.

Connection and closeness are good—but not at the expense of necessary rules. As Sissy Goff says, having our teenagers respect us is more important than having them like us. "We've all heard the old sayings that rules without relationship lead to rebellion," she says, "but we'd like to add that relationship without rules leads to kids feeling too much power and a lack of safety. The goal is to work toward having rules and relationship in place, and to parent consistently with both."[25]

Teenagers have plenty of buddies, she adds, but only one set of parents. When we "buddy parent," we lose their respect and often set them up to feel insecure.[26]

Additionally, permissive parents who try to be their teenager's BFF often hurt their child as positive influences pull away and the wilder crowd gravitates to them.

Psychologist Dr. Lisa Damour says this about setting limits:

> Why do teenagers move on to risky business when they don't meet resistance on the small stuff? Because teens want to know where the lines are and that they'll be called out of bounds if they cross them. . . . Indeed, research has long established that teens whose parents are highly permissive—where they are indulgent, neglectful, or just reluctant to step in—are more likely to abuse substances and misbehave at school than teens whose parents articulate and enforce limits.[27]

Teenagers crave freedom and need freedom to make good choices. As parents, we work toward the reality that in most states, teenagers are recognized as legal adults at age eighteen. Keeping too tight a leash can prevent your daughter from building muscles of self-control, but letting her run loose can be a disaster. How do you extend more freedom and impose consequences when trust is broken? How do you keep a relationship without losing control?

Every family is unique, but one universal truth is that disciplining only works when done in *love*, not anger. When you're angry, it's best to cool down, pray, and get your mind in a rational place before acting.

After all, anger can be a grenade. As Dr. Gary Chapman says, "In more than thirty years of marriage and family counseling, I have often wept as teenagers have recounted the painful words and destructive behavior of parents whose anger was out of control. What is even more tragic is the many young adults who were abused as teenagers and now find themselves treating their own children in the same manner their parents treated them."[28]

Many teenagers feel like their parents are never satisfied. They believe their parents care more about their grades and accomplishments than their well-being and emotional health. Being aware of this common pitfall can help you avoid it. Even if your daughter stumbles, you can show her you care while holding her accountable.

My friend who got drunk in high school, for instance, said his dad walked in on him vomiting in the toilet. He didn't say a word; instead, his father gave him water and helped him into bed. He made sure he was okay. Early the next morning, his father woke him up with a special job: to mow the grass of their very large lawn. The smell of grass combined with a hangover made my friend throw up more, and when he finished, his dad sat him down and calmly said, "You want to talk about last night, son?" From there he made his point, and because my friend had great respect for his dad and wanted to please him, he took every word to heart.

In contrast, teenagers won't take our words to heart if we expect more of them than we do of ourselves. They hate hypocrisy, so if we tell them not to get drunk and then stumble home wasted ourselves, we lose credibility. We erode the relationship when they need it most.

Your daughter has it harder than you did at her age. She needs your guidance, your wisdom, your rules, and your consequences. Without a relationship, she won't listen, but with a relationship, she will. Offer correction in love, and aim for measured responses. Challenge her and cheer for her, setting expectations that help her grow while embracing her humanity as a sister in Christ.

Discipline your children, and they will give you peace of mind and will make your heart glad.

—PROVERBS 29:17 NLT

MODEL GOD'S MERCY

"We live in a society where everything is permissible, but nothing is forgivable."[29]

This truth, from Reverend Andrew Pearson, explains the dichotomy of the world shaping our daughters. First, they are told that "anything goes." Then when they make a mistake and cross some invisible line, they are labeled, condemned, and shamed.

Thankfully, God's ways and thoughts are higher. While God certainly sets a high bar, calling us to live like Jesus, He knows we'll miss the mark repeatedly. He's aware that our rock-bottom moments open the door to His mercy. His kindness when we least deserve it (or expect it) helps turn us away from our sin. It convicts us in life-changing ways.

"We think that we are saved when we get it right," says Father Joseph Corpora, "when we stop sinning, when we become perfect. But the exact opposite is the truth. God saves us through our sins, through our imperfections, through our faults, through our failings, through our weaknesses. God saves us as sinners, not as saints."[30]

When your daughter fails—and she will—walk with her through the fallout. Remember how we are all just one bad decision away from stepping off a cliff. The big question is not "Will my daughter mess up?" but rather "How will I respond when she messes up? Will I reject her or show her love?"

Your daughter won't learn about mercy from a merciless world, so teach it at home. Share the parable of the prodigal son. Emphasize God's grace. Admit your mistakes and tell her how God carried you through them. Criticize your daughter's poor behavior and poor choices but not your daughter as a person. Ask her how she'd handle the situation if she could do it over again, and remind her that who she's becoming matters more than who she's been in the past.

How you respond to your daughter's mistakes can deepen your relationship or destroy it. Even when discipline is needed, you can present it in a way that builds hope and trust. No matter what she does, or how unforgivable her mistakes appear in the world's opinion, you can parent her with love and mercy, taking your cues from a God who gives us all more than we deserve.

———————— • ————————

Blessed are the merciful, for they will be shown mercy.

–MATTHEW 5:7

———————— • ————————

TIME + MATURITY = PERSPECTIVE

A former high school baseball coach told me about a phone call he received a few years ago. It came from a player who is now in his thirties. As a high school junior, this player lost his spot on the team after failing a drug test. He called his former coach to thank him for showing tough love because it forced him to get his act together. It enabled him to later become a successful (and wealthy) entrepreneur.

Today is just a moment in time. What seems unfair to your daughter now will make more sense down the road. While many teenagers won't need extreme measures, there are times (like when lives are at risk) when they need to know that their parents mean business.

I can't promise that your daughter will sing your praises one day or apologize for giving you grief. I can tell you, however, that listening to God brings peace. In a world of instant gratification, where immediate payoff is king, it helps to remember that shaping a child's heart is a long journey. We aren't guaranteed rewards in this life, but if we're faithful, God will reward us in heaven.

Love wants what is best for your daughter long term. Love can help her become a healthy, thriving adult. Love cares more about her relationship with God than whether you look like a rock star and model parent.

Love your daughter as God loves you, and prepare her for the day when she must stand on her own two feet. Cultivate an inner strength that may ultimately become the best gift you ever gave her.

Thanks be to God! He gives us the victory through our Lord Jesus Christ.

—1 CORINTHIANS 15:57

REFLECTION QUESTIONS

1. How comfortable are you with your daughter being upset if you *know* you've made the right choice? Do you ever cave to stay in her good graces? Explain.

2. What choices did your parents make that taught you to stand on your own two feet? Did you like your parents at the time? Did you say, "I will not be *that* parent"?

3. Compare your opinion of your mom when you were sixteen years old versus age thirty or forty. Did time and maturity alter your perspective? Why or why not?

4. What comes more naturally to you: setting rules for your daughter or building a relationship with her? How can you strike a healthy balance?

5. What is the hardest part of parenting a teenager today?

6. When your daughter messes up, what is your response? Describe a time when you showed mercy and a time when you showed tough love.

MAKE YOUR RELATIONSHIP A PRIORITY

When you are in the final days of your life, what will you want? Will you hug that college degree in the walnut frame? Will you ask to be carried to the garage so you can sit in your car? Will you find comfort in rereading your financial statement? Of course not. What will matter then will be people. If relationships will matter most then, shouldn't they matter most now?
–MAX LUCADO[1]

Three working moms I know recently cut back on their business hours to spend more time with their teenagers.

Another mom with five kids gets a babysitter for her two-year-old so she can drive her fourteen-year-old to activities.

While her baby needs basic love and nurturing, her teenager has emotional needs that are best met by someone who knows her well.

These moms are different, yet their choices evolved from the same realization: their children need them more in the teenage years, and they want to be available.

It is deceiving, isn't it? When we look at teenagers, we see self-sufficiency, independence, and a desire to be with friends. Teenagers can drive, make their own breakfast, and self-advocate with teachers. They can work jobs, juggle five tests and two papers in one week, and travel abroad.

On the surface, it seems like all teens require is food, shelter, money, and car rides until their sixteenth birthday. In many ways, they don't need their parents like they did as young children.

Below the surface, however, are invisible needs. Teenagers face tough situations and make big life choices that call for guidance, support, love, and security. The parents who once wiped their bottoms, cut their food into bite-size pieces, and rocked them to sleep are still needed—in less obvious but still significant ways. Parents wear new hats and take on new roles such as these:

- counselor
- adviser
- coach
- mentor
- consultant
- collaborator
- cheerleader
- encourager
- teacher

Moms often ask me, "How do I get my daughter to open up? How do I make her listen? I want her to tell me everything, and I have so much to teach her, but she tunes me out."

I understand the frustration, and I've certainly felt that disconnect. How do you become your daughter's counselor? How do you earn a voice in her life—and gain her trust and respect? How do you keep a rapport that makes her feel comfortable sharing her life and struggles?

The key is to grow a relationship. Teenagers are very relational, and as they grow up, parents go from being in a position of *power* to a position of *influence*. We can't control them, but we can show them we care by putting time, effort, and thought into knowing them.

In *The Back Door to Your Teen's Heart*, Sissy Goff writes, "We've found that the quickest way to be dismissed by an adolescent is to try to be a part of their lives without establishing a real relationship with them. As we try to enter into the life of a teenager, establishing an authentic relationship is crucial."[2]

Too often we try to pop into a teenager's life when it's convenient (or when they need a lesson or punishment) and expect to be heard. We forget how they are human and, like any human, they prefer to listen to people who regularly engage in their lives.

Growing a relationship with your daughter will look unique because God works through your unique circumstances. Not all moms have the luxury or the desire to cut back their work hours or curtail their commitments. Some moms start a new career in the teen years because they need money to pay for college, they have a sudden financial crisis, they are single or widowed, or they have more free time and want to invest in themselves. Every family is different, and what matters most is making time for your daughter during a challenging season.

God rewards faithfulness, and you never know what will come from the efforts you make today. Even if you don't see immediate rewards, you can find peace in knowing that any seeds of love you plant won't go to waste.

———————— • ————————

Let us not become weary in doing good, for at the proper time we will reap a harvest if we do not give up.

–GALATIANS 6:9

———————— • ————————

THE TRUTH IS A GIFT, EVEN WHEN IT HURTS

It is often easier to be honest with people we barely know than with the people we know best.

Why? Because our lives aren't intertwined with the lives of strangers. We have nothing to lose by being honest. If a conversation goes south or they think we're crazy, we can simply walk away.

The closer we are to someone, the more courage it takes to be fully honest. When we know what makes them angry or sad . . . when we can predict their reactions . . . when we're scared of damaging the relationship or hurting their feelings . . . when we feel worried that they may think less of us or withdraw their love . . . it's tempting to edit the truth or lie.

But relationships need honesty to grow stronger and deeper. Being lied to is painful, and as you've most likely experienced in your life, it takes time to rebuild trust.

Any relationship that stands the test of time will have ups and downs. One thing I tell my daughters is how important honesty is to me, even if I'm not happy about the news. I want them to be honest when they mess up, honest about their problems, and honest about their needs. I'd rather know now if there's something they wish I'd do—like use a gentler tone or listen without giving advice—than wait twenty years to learn about their secret desires.

Recently my daughter expressed honesty that caught my husband and me off guard. What began as a talk about her cell phone led to a talk about our parenting. She said that lately she'd felt resentful toward us.

It wasn't an easy admission. She had tears in her eyes as she told us. We told her that we appreciated her honesty and hoped that she'd keep talking. We value her thoughts and feelings. We have to be her parents, but we also want open communication that helps us find the most effective approach.

After all, we're learning as we go. There is no perfect playbook on raising teens, and anyone who insists they have all the answers is someone I don't trust.

Sometimes our approach to parenting needs an overhaul, and sometimes it just needs tweaks. Like the disciples in John 21:6, who fished all night and caught nothing and then took Jesus' advice to throw their nets on the other side of the boat and caught more fish than they could haul in, we need Jesus' voice in our lives. If we listen and obey, He'll point us toward choices that give life. He'll tell us what pivots are needed to find the sweet spot we're searching for.

Relationships need respectful honesty, not brutal honesty, to go from bad to good or from good to great. The truth that hurts can also heal if we let God show the way.

"You will know the truth, and the truth will set you free."

–JOHN 8:32 NLT

DEEPEN YOUR CONNECTION

People often talk about teen girls like they're all nightmares. Many conversations and articles about teen girls only perpetuate this mindset.

I'm not a Pollyanna, and I know the words often used to describe this demographic—*self-centered, dramatic, gossipy, clueless, moody, rude, angsty, forgetful, sassy, mean*—hold truth in certain moments and interactions.

It bothers me, however, when we settle for this script and believe this stage of a girl's life is hopeless. Society conditions us to expect the worst, and for too many people the attitude becomes, "Teenage girls are difficult and fight constantly with their moms. . . . What can anybody do?"

Actually, there is a lot we can do. Relationships take work, and even when we disagree with our daughters, we can learn to disagree well and find healthy ways to work through conflict. We can refuse to accept that their final years at home must be miserable or tense.

Here are ideas to enhance that connection.

Twenty Ways to Grow a Relationship with Your Teen Daughter

1. Take the lead.

Your daughter's mind is a whirlwind of thoughts and worries, and chances are, she thinks more about friends, school, boys, and life than she thinks about you. If there's a problem, it's up to *you* to make the first move. You can't change her, but you can change your response to her and establish a new dynamic.

Mother Angelica said,

"Not getting along with someone is a two-way street, and many times if one of you is willing to change, the whole relationship can change. I think that's true of any kind of friendship, particularly with negative personalities. Somebody has to get in there and begin the healing. As long as two people are fighting nothing good will happen—and we shouldn't expect the other person to change first."[3]

I've been through rough patches with three teenage daughters. What always helps me is to (1) give it time and be patient as necessary struggles play out and (2) do my part. Rough patches drive me to God and amplify my prayer life. They remind me to trust Him with the heart work and legwork that can lead me and my daughters to a better place.

2. Learn from your mistakes.

I'm a creature of habit, so I like routines, but I'm learning to adjust my sails when I notice unhealthy dynamics with my teenagers.

It's often through mistakes that I find a better way. I take note of what helps my relationship with my girls (disciplining out of love, explaining the logic behind rules and boundaries, standing strong and united with my husband, apologizing when I'm wrong, pointing out their strengths, using humor when possible, showing empathy, and listening) and what hurts the relationship (disciplining out of anger, getting too lax or lazy, excessive questioning, criticizing, yelling, and not listening). Though every child is different, some actions work across the board. They are all rooted in love and focus on long-term well-being.

3. Be concise.

Once my girls became teenagers, they stopped listening after thirty seconds of any "life lesson" I gave.

Apparently, this is common. Another mom of four girls said that her oldest daughter told her, "I like going to Dad when I need advice because he is more concise."

Ouch! (Did I mention how a sense of humor is a must when raising teens?)

Generally speaking, men are more concise. Brevity is their strength, and while some women are certainly succinct, many of us get chatty. We unload too many thoughts at once, and the gems get lost in the shuffle. Rather than deliver dissertations, I aim to be brief, sharing key truths in ten words or less.

I also aim to ask fewer (and better) questions. As a mom ahead of me admitted, her daughter shuts down if she probes too deeply on any given subject. Their running joke is, "That's three questions, Mom. You've hit your limit." This mom has learned to carefully consider the three questions she's allowed to ask.

Since teenagers are busy, your time with your daughter is valuable. Talking in shorter spurts ensures that your message is heard and gives her a chance to speak. This allows wisdom to flow both ways and builds a trust that can lead to deeper and longer dialogue.

4. Let go of regret.

We all have regrets—or things we wish we'd done better—but what matters more than the past is how we move forward.

Even if your relationship with your daughter is shaky, even if you fear that you've been too strict or not strict enough, even if your heart is broken because you showed tough love and now she won't speak to you, there is hope. God's love is bigger than any argument, silent treatment, or bad season, and there is nothing He can't repair.

As we read in the book of Job, God allowed Satan to test Job's faith by taking away everything except his life. Job lost his family, his wealth, his health, and everything he cared about. He faced catastrophe after catastrophe and struggled with God. Miraculously, Job stayed faithful, and God blessed the last part of Job's life more than the first part.

Again, God rewards faithfulness (either here or in heaven) and specializes in miracles. Don't ruin today by ruminating on yesterday. Instead, let the past inspire today's choices, and be thankful for the second chance you get each morning.

5. Don't compare your relationship to that of other moms and daughters.

We all do this, right? Even if we know better, we notice how other moms and daughters interact—*Are they affectionate? Close? Loving and respectful? Happy together?*—and we then feel better or worse in comparison.

But relationships are unique. They are fluid and change daily. What you observe is a snapshot in time, and while some mothers and daughters are clearly closer than others, every relationship has peaks, valleys, hard seasons, and hidden tensions. A good relationship is never stagnant because it constantly adapts to new seasons. What may be a terrific season for one family could be torture for another.

Personalities also play a role. An extroverted girl may tell her mom everything because she can't keep it in. An introverted girl may tell her mom nothing because she can't get it out. A girl with sisters or close friends may turn to them for advice. A girl with all brothers or shaky friendships may find solidarity with her mom.

A young mom whom I consider a role model for my daughters

told me that when she was in high school, there was a season when she wasn't close to her mom. Her friends who were close to their moms during this time were wild. They told their moms everything because their moms allowed drinking and other activities in order to keep open communication.

"I realize now that my mom sacrificed that closeness with me," this young mom said. "I appreciate it now, but I couldn't then."

Many factors can affect the mother-daughter relationship. More important than your daughter telling you *everything* is your daughter knowing she can tell you *anything*—feeling so secure in your love that she's willing to come to you with problems, struggles, or secrets. Rather than make other moms your benchmark, let God foster an authentic connection that suits you and your daughter.

6. Give her space.

I used to get my feelings hurt if my daughters wanted time alone in their bedrooms or if they came home from school and didn't want to talk.

Now I realize this is normal. Teenagers need space, and they're developing identities apart from their families. After a long day, they aren't always in the mood to chat.

Sometimes what your daughter needs is a snack and room to decompress. Rather than pepper her with questions, you can back off and leave the ball in her court. Allowing her to talk on her terms, when she's relaxed and rested, will breed a more natural conversation than one that is forced.

7. Spend one-on-one time together.

I grew up in a family of five children, and now I'm raising four kids. I believe in having one-on-one time with each child.

It doesn't have to be planned, and most of my one-on-one time isn't. With my girls, I take advantage of pockets of time. If someone has a doctor's appointment, we might grab Starbucks before checking back into school. If there's a movie someone loves, I'll ask if she wants to watch it one night at home. If I feel disconnected from one child, I'll invite her out for frozen yogurt, dinner, or shopping.

For my girls' tenth and sixteenth birthdays, I take them to New York for a weekend. We go with close friends and their mothers before Christmas, and it's worth every penny I save to make it happen. Having a few days of uninterrupted time—laughing, exploring a city, and treating my daughter like an only child—helps us bond in new ways and allows me to see my daughter's personality away from the influence of siblings.

One-on-one time doesn't have to be fancy. It could mean going to the grocery store to get ingredients for a new recipe, taking a walk to reach a Fitbit goal, or snuggling on the couch. It's anything that makes your daughter feel singled out and not lost in the shuffle.

8. Express what you love about her.

I always loved it when my mother pointed out my strengths. Growing up, she told me I was creative and had a gift for writing. She suggested public relations as my college major because I was organized and good at planning. My mother said I was coachable, able to take feedback and run with it, and she explained how this quality would take me far in life. She also told me that I'd only get better with time, peaking later in life, not early, because of my potential and work ethic.

Clearly, her comments stuck. They shaped how I saw myself, and they boosted my confidence.

Whatever strengths you see in your daughter, point them out. Even if she looks like she's not listening, she'll be touched by your observations.

9. Protect her privacy.

I once asked my daughter what helped her make a good choice in a tricky situation. She credited an older cousin and advice he once shared.

I thanked this cousin and didn't think anything of it until my daughter sent me a text to ask if I'd told anyone about her tricky situation. Apparently, this cousin—with good intentions—had texted her an extra word of encouragement, and my daughter felt betrayed that I didn't keep that conversation between us.

This was a lesson for me. Teenagers value their privacy, and as parents we earn their trust. If you're not careful with what you say or who you share things with—even with good intentions—your daughter may shut you out.

10. Make her a priority.

A woman's spiritual director told her, "Life is a series of trade-offs. With everything you add to your list, you have to take something off."

The trade-offs that cost you the most can potentially add the most value. Rather than doing it all, make room for delayed gratification. Put first things first, focusing on what must be done now and saving the rest for another season.

You only get one chance to raise your daughter. You only have her at home for eighteen years, a fraction of her life. What happens in this period sets the stage for your long-term adult relationship. By making yourself available during the limited time you have left, you deepen your relationship's roots.

The most important things in life, like relationships, are rarely urgent, and that's why it's imperative to make time for them. At the end of the day, the two things that matter most are your faith and your family, and it is worth making sacrifices for both.

11. Show affection, even if she doesn't reciprocate.

When my daughter was twelve, she picked up a new habit that baffled me. When she was tired or had just woken up, she'd stand in front of me, drop her head, and be quiet. If I asked a question, she'd mumble or shrug. I knew she wanted something, but what?

Then one day it hit me. I noticed how her body was leaning in, ever so slightly, and waiting for a response. What she wanted was something I hadn't given in a while: a hug. So, I wrapped my arms around her tired body and held her, and though she didn't hug me back, I knew my instincts were correct when she leaned into my hug and relaxed.

Clearly, there is a time and a place to hug your teenage daughter, and it's not usually in front of her friends. Kids of all ages need physical touch from their parents, and whether it's a hug, a kiss, a high five, a fist bump, or a pat on the back, these gestures convey that your daughter is seen and loved.

12. Own up to your flaws.

I used to believe I had to be a perfect role model for my girls. I thought that admitting my flaws would make them think less of me, so I didn't do it.

As they grew up, they became harder to fool. They started to see my flaws, so when I pretended not to have any, they were wisely skeptical.

Teenagers appreciate honesty. As we own up to our shortcomings—saying things like, "You know what? My impatience caused me to be rude to that cashier, and I need to work on that"—they start to trust us more. They learn how to look inward and practice self-reflection too.

This is significant because it goes against their tendencies. As neuroscientist Dr. Frances Jensen explains, "Pride and image are big for teens, and they are not able to look into themselves and be self-critical."[4] By being honest about yourself, you teach your daughter to bravely do the same.

13. Show up, keep trying, and do your best.

My dad has always told me, "Do your best, Kari, and leave the results to God." It's a motto you can apply to anything—even parenting.

The truth is, we like tidy results. We want a rainbow at the end of the storm, an agreeable answer to a prayer, an outcome that reflects the blood, sweat, and tears we invested.

But relationships are not so cut-and-dried. Sometimes the rewards are immediate, and sometimes they're delayed. Sometimes prayers get answered much differently than we hoped for. Sometimes people surprise us in the best and worst ways.

You can't control your daughter, but you can control your attitude, actions, and choices. Do these things well, with patience and humility, and remember the best work isn't done in a hurry. If you do what God calls you to do, you can leave the outcome to Him.

14. Be the driver.

My best conversations with my teens often happen in the car, which is helpful since we're in the car a lot. If you live in a city with public transportation, you can use that as your "car time" as well.

I love car time for the following reasons:

- **I have my daughter's undivided attention, and she has mine.** Unlike home, the car doesn't require a juggling act. I'm not distracted by laundry, dishes, and emails. My only job is to drive, which frees my mind and makes me more attentive to what my teenager says.

- Picking my daughter up from school or activities allows me to catch raw thoughts and emotions. I can sense, by the way my daughter approaches my car, whether school or an activity was good or not. I love being the first to hear about an accomplishment or a disappointment, and even those car rides where she bursts into tears can lead to important dialogue and life lessons.
- Driving enables one-on-one interaction. Even a five-minute drive to practice allows me to tell my daughter how proud I am of her.
- Not facing each other makes it easier to have brave and honest conversations. I learned in a psychology class that looking at someone can make you lose your courage or say what *they* want to hear. With a teenager, the car can be especially conducive to having a difficult or awkward talk.
- Having a teenager requires new ways to connect. Gone are the days when my daughter talks to me as I tuck her into bed. Most nights she is up later than I am to finish her homework, so having car time helps me keep a pulse on her life.

Most moms don't want to be the driver shuttling teenagers around, but you can learn a lot by simply listening to your daughter and her closest friends as they talk. With multiple voices chiming in, you'll hear about class dynamics, crushes, and breaking news.

15. Listen and occasionally negotiate.

Dr. Lisa Damour says, "When teens are trapped with parents who would rather flaunt their power than negotiate on even minor points, it doesn't always end so well. These parents don't just damage their relationships with their daughters, they can also provoke girls into proving that they will not be controlled."[5]

In short, nobody likes a dictator. Nobody feels close to a parent who stays on a power trip.

Recently, two people told me about a parochial school from which the graduates are notorious for going wild in college. The school's spiritual foundation does not cause the rebellion, because instilling truth in children is crucial. But what can stir up rebellion is teenagers feeling so sheltered, controlled, or pressured to be perfect that they can't wait to escape. When any human being feels pushed to an extreme, it's only a matter of time before the pendulum swings the opposite way.

Sometimes after listening to your teenager explain why she's asking for a privilege, you may change your mind. If she has proven to be a responsible driver, you may agree she's ready to drive to a concert in a neighboring town. If she asks to go to the lake with friends, and she's made good choices in the past and will be with a mom you trust, you may let her go. If she has three tests on Monday and maintains good grades without nagging or supervision from you, you may let her attend a Sunday night birthday party.

Your daughter is less likely to fight your nonnegotiable decisions if you negotiate on occasion. By giving her more leeway as she shows maturity—and giving consequences if she mishandles it—you're preparing her for life as an adult.

16. Teach her to work through conflict.

Most girls are not taught how to work through conflict, but they should be. As a writer for teens, I can attest that most heartache in a girl's life relates to conflict with friends: friends being mean, writing friends off, being passive-aggressive, and not showing loyalty.

Some girls avoid conflict at all costs and become doormats. Other girls are so blunt and confrontational that they turn people off. There is a place in the middle where healthy debate can occur, and as a mom, you help your daughter find it.

In his book *Welcome to Adulting*, pastor Jonathan Pokluda says that an ability to resolve conflict is one of life's most valuable skills.

> Since life is so heavily focused on relationships, and relationships always involve conflict, how you resolve those conflicts will have a huge impact on how happy you are. It can even alter the direction of your life in big ways. For example, the number-one predictor of success in marriage is how well the two of you can resolve conflict. An inability to resolve conflict can cost you friends, cost you jobs, and keep you from having peace.[6]

When you and your daughter argue, consider it a learning experience. As your daughter expresses her thoughts and feelings, she'll grow in assertiveness. As she listens to your perspective, she'll gain empathy. As she speaks the truth in love, she'll discover the power of finding the right words.

Together these skills can grow her relationship with you and teach her how to reconcile her problems with others. They turn arguments into life lessons and set her up for success in every relationship—even marriage.

17. Apologize.

A genuine apology can go a long way. I don't apologize unless I mean it, because that would be manipulative, but what God reveals to me through apologies is the power of righting a wrong. It softens hearts, brings down guards, and redirects the conversation.

I've seen shock on my daughter's face when I've offered an

apology she didn't expect. She was surprised, for instance, when I apologized for making a negative remark about her friend who had made disappointing choices. It had made my daughter angry and defensive, and with some reflection, I realized I'd be angry and defensive, too, if she point-blank verbalized one of my friend's flaws.

If your apologies feel awkward or come through gritted teeth, it's okay. Most of us aren't pros, and you've got to start somewhere. The goal, I believe, is to repair any damage you've caused or provoked. Life is too short to be stubborn, and when you look back in ten years, you'll regret the apologies you held back from your daughter more than the apologies you gave.

18. Forgive.

In any family relationship, there are a lifetime of interactions. This leaves a lot of room for error and conversations that can go wrong. Over time the little hurts add up. They grow into resentments that make us bitter or distant.

The only way to avoid bitterness is to stay softhearted like Jesus. This is difficult (especially when your daughter makes you feel unappreciated, disrespected, or unloved), but as Matthew 6:14–15 says, as we forgive others, that's how God forgives us.

Recently my daughter argued with me about her upcoming birthday party. She had her heart set on going to a haunted house, but since some friends would be too scared, we needed an alternative. She grew irritable as I threw out suggestions, and it took me several deep breaths to stay calm and not catalog every time she'd acted this way. Instead of letting this build up as anger in my heart, I let it go.

The next day she felt terrible and apologized. I forgave her, hugged her, and told her I still love her even when she acts salty. We talked about emotions and laughed about how far she's come since her fifth-grade angsty stage. We agreed that we all say things out of frustration, and the important thing is to learn from our mistakes, apologize, and move on.

19. Don't take rejection personally.

In her book *Untangled*, Dr. Lisa Damour compares teenage daughters to swimmers who need to explore the water of the broader world. Parents are like the edge of the pool where girls catch their breath and recover.

When something goes wrong, she says, your daughter may swim to you, asking for advice, showing affection, and sharing details of her life. You're in heaven, but just as you think you've gotten her back, she returns to the water to swim. She gets there by pushing off the side of the pool because lingering too long feels babyish, and that's the last thing a normal teenager wants to feel when parting with childhood.

Dr. Damour explains:

> Your daughter needs a wall to swim to, and she needs you to be a wall that can withstand her comings and goings. Some parents feel too hurt by their swimmers, take too personally their daughter's rejections, and choose to make themselves unavailable to avoid going through it again. . . . But being unavailable comes at a cost. Unavailable parents miss out on some wonderful, if brief, moments with their daughters. Worse, their daughters are left without a wall to swim to and must navigate choppy—and sometimes dangerous—waters all on their own.[7]

Dr. Damour says to enjoy your daughter when she swims to you, but anticipate the push off. Brace yourself for the rejection that can come on the heels of overdue closeness, and don't let her mistreat you as she pushes off. Though it hurts when warm moments quickly turn cold, there are benefits as your daughter learns independence.

20. Have fun together.

Parenting can be exhausting, and the season of adolescence can feel like a hamster wheel, the same routine repeated day after day. Break the monotony when possible. Dance in the kitchen, blare music in the car, and make your daughter laugh. Even if she rolls her eyes, she'll enjoy the comic relief. One day when you're gone, these memories of your silly side may provoke the biggest smiles.

You know your daughter best, and these ideas are just a starting point. Decide what speaks to your girl, and then look for ways to engage with her world.

———————— • ————————

As iron sharpens iron, so one person sharpens another.

—PROVERBS 27:17

———————— • ————————

IT WILL NEVER BE PERFECT

Chances are, you've felt disheartened at times by your relationship with your daughter.

When you snuggled with her as a baby and dreamed of the future, you may have imagined dance parties, tea parties, dress up, shopping, manicures, movie nights, and late-night chats. You pictured mother-daughter bonding that united you for life.

While many dreams manifested, others did not. With each stage came new challenges and pushback that widened the gulf between fantasy and reality. At some point you made a choice: you could wait for perfection or adjust your expectations.

Soon after my husband and I got engaged, we attended marriage counseling through my church. The leaders spent an entire session talking about *disillusionment*. In any long-term commitment, they said, disillusionment is normal. You'll have periods of doubt and days when you wonder if you made the right choice. If you work through the disappointment, you'll get stronger. You'll grow a more honest and deeper relationship free from illusions and false expectations.

Issues are inevitable when two flawed people do life together. While you can build a great relationship with your daughter, it's unrealistic to expect perfection, especially as you're parenting her. If perfection is your goal, you'll end up disillusioned.

Set aside notions of what your relationship "should" or "could" look like, and trust God's vision. Ask Him to work through your circumstances and help you grow Christlike love. Make memories with your daughter, and build a solid relationship that can grow more layered and real with time.

———————— • ————————

"I am the vine; you are the branches. If you remain in me and I in you, you will bear much fruit; apart from me you can do nothing."

—JOHN 15:5

———————— • ————————

REFLECTION QUESTIONS

. . . .

1. Has anyone tried to advise you without getting to know you first? Did you trust or listen to the person? Why or why not?

2. What is unique about your relationship with your daughter? How is God working through your current circumstances, even if they're not ideal?

3. Has your daughter ever given you feedback that you took to heart? If so, what happened when you made changes? Did your relationship grow stronger?

4. Think of a time when you felt disillusionment with your daughter, disappointed that a moment fell short of expectations. What did you learn about fantasy versus reality?

5. Pride can ruin the parent-teen relationship. Has pride ever kept you from admitting when you were wrong? Are there past incidents you should apologize for to root out any resentment between you and your daughter?

6. What fun memory from your childhood can you replicate with your daughter now?

SEE THE GOOD, LOVING HER *AS* SHE IS AND *WHERE* SHE IS

We rarely see people as they really are; our perceptions are distorted by past relationships and our own preconceptions of who we think they are, even the people we know best. We do not see clearly because of the "logs" in our eyes (Matt. 7:3–5).
–DR. HENRY CLOUD AND DR. JOHN TOWNSEND[1]

When I was thirteen years old, I was vain and self-centered. I spent an hour getting ready for school each morning. I thought about myself obsessively.

My only goal was to be a model or famous actress, which I pursued by sending in monthly pictures to the *Teen Magazine* Model Search (I never made the cut).

When I made the cheer squad and my two best friends didn't, it never occurred to me how disappointed they might feel because I felt so happy.

And then there was my babysitting business—inspired not by my love of kids but by my love for fashion and the need for cash to stay trendy.

In short, I lived in a bubble. I thought the universe revolved around *me*. While I was kindhearted and friendly to others, I had a lot of growing up to do. I was a typical teenager: self-conscious, self-critical, and overly concerned with people's opinions of me.

I had to jog these memories as I started to write for teen girls. It took me several attempts to find the right voice, until one day my editor told me, "If you sound like a mom, the girls will stop reading. Write instead like a big sister or wise best friend. Remember yourself at their age. Channel your teenage self."

It sounded fun—at first—to channel my teenage self. But as I dug into my past and unburied forgotten memories, I started to cringe and want a do-over. Chances are, you have memories from your past that make you cringe as well. Events or remarks that you aren't proud of and wish you could undo.

If you take a minute to think about them and consider how far you've come, it will soften your heart toward your daughter. You may find extra patience for dealing with the temporary flaws you see right now.

Your daughter is a work in progress, just like you and me. Who she is at age thirteen, sixteen, or even twenty-six is not who she will be as a mature adult. Beneath the vanity and self-absorption commonly seen in teenagers is a diamond in the rough. There is a deeply impressionable girl whom God is still working on—and who craves the unshakable love of her mother in every stage and season.

I am certain that God, who began the good work within you, will continue his work until it is finally finished on the day when Christ Jesus returns.

—PHILIPPIANS 1:6 NLT

RECOGNIZE HER POTENTIAL

Michelangelo was an Italian artist who created brilliant masterpieces. Two of his most famous sculptures—*David*, from the biblical David and Goliath account, and the *Pietà*—he sculpted before he turned thirty.

Clearly, Michelangelo was gifted with his hands. But he also had the gift of vision, and during an anniversary trip to Italy, my husband and I learned about the vision that inspired his magnificent work.

In Florence's Accademia Gallery, which hosts Michelangelo's *David* sculpture and many half-finished sculptures, our tour guide told us that when Michelangelo looked at a slab of marble, he saw a figure hiding inside who wanted to be set free. His philosophy was to chip away the marble to uncover that hidden figure.

"Every block of stone has a statue inside it," Michelangelo said, "and it is the task of the sculptor to discover it."[2]

When God looks at us, He sees that hidden masterpiece. He notices the inner potential that nobody else can see yet. And like a brilliant sculptor who chips away stone, He removes our hard edges. If we trust His hand and vision, He'll transform us into something more beautiful than we ever dared to imagine.

Currently, your daughter is like Michelangelo's half-finished sculptures. You may see glimpses of her potential, but only God sees the final masterpiece. Only God with His perfect vision can see the full picture of who she's meant to become as time and life events shape her.

One prayer you can pray is, "Lord, help me see her through Your eyes. Help me love her like You do. Show me her potential."

You get a front-row seat to the sculpting of your daughter's life. You witness every chip, every victory, every heartache. Be the first to believe in her and the last to lose faith. Don't wait until she is perfect to love her, because it's the love you show her today—even as she acts tough, distant, or ornery—that helps crack the shell around her hidden potential.

That is what the Scriptures mean when they say, "No eye has seen, no ear has heard, and no mind has imagined what God has prepared for those who love him."

–1 CORINTHIANS 2:9 NLT

SEE THE GOOD

We live in a world that thrives on negativity. We have all-day news channels devoted to doom and gloom. We see viral videos that bust people for misbehaving. We're drawn to train wrecks, and thanks to technology, we can catch people at their worst and publicize what happened—even ten years after the fact.

But here's what rarely gets attention: catching people at their best. Celebrating what people do right. Changing someone's heart as they realize how good it feels to be seen in a positive light.

I've been as guilty as any mom of trying to "perfect" my teenagers. A ticking clock inside my head tells me time is running out; I have only a few more years to "fix" them and prepare them for life. The pressure feels intense because their future is on the line, and as I watch other parents launch their kids, I feel an urgency in my heart.

This triggers anxiety in me. It makes me spring into action before going to God in prayer and asking Him to take the lead.

I've also been guilty of seeing my daughters as extensions of me. At times I project my thoughts, emotions, and experiences on them. I want to save them from my mistakes and heartaches, give them opportunities I wish I'd had, and calm my fears by taking control.

As I do this, I miss who *they* are. When I treat my daughters as my second chance, I fail to see them as unique individuals meant to live their own lives.

Sissy Goff and Melissa Trevathan, in their book *The Back Door to Your Teen's Heart*, explain a common mother-daughter dynamic:

> Adolescent daughters bring to light the insecurities of their mothers . . . For women, the insecurity can turn into a critical view of their daughters. Mothers often see their daughters as extensions of themselves. They expect their daughters to be a perfected version of themselves.[3]

Wow. Profound, right? The truth hurts, but facing uncomfortable truths is where real growth begins. Nobody wants a mother who is never satisfied, and nobody enjoys the company of someone who expects perfection.

So how do we do our job as moms, setting a high yet realistic bar, and still make our daughters feel loved? How do we see the good as we deal with eye rolls, attitudes, selfishness, mood swings, a critical spirit, power struggles, sass, or the urge to ground them for the rest of their lives?

We do it by stepping away from the microscope to see the

bigger picture. Here are some thoughts to help us attain that point of view.

Ten Ways to See the Good in Your Daughter

1. Be quick to point out what she does right.

When your daughter takes a step in the right direction, applaud her. Let her know that you see her helping her brother with a math problem, laughing with the neighbor, putting away laundry, playing her heart out in a game, or working hard on a project. Even praise like "Your brother is lucky to have a sister like you" or "You showed class tonight and made me so proud" will stick with her and impact her self-image and future choices.

2. Love her as she is.

I've heard it said, "Raise the child you have, not the child you want." This is great advice because many of us go into parenting with preconceived notions and fantasies. We want our kids to be like us, only better. Since God has a sense of humor, He often gives us the opposite. A social butterfly mom may have an introverted daughter. Super-athletic parents may have a child who enjoys art and poetry.

When you can celebrate your daughter's personality without wishing for her to change or be more like you, that's a pivotal parenting moment.

I have a friend whose daughter was diagnosed with cancer when she went for her pediatric checkup at two years old. She is healthy now and in remission, but it was a scary time.

Before the diagnosis, this little girl's spunk and strong personality frustrated her mother. She wanted her to be calm and easygoing. After the diagnosis, however, her mom realized how God made her feisty for a reason. She needed a special armor to handle the grueling treatments needed to fight cancer as a two-year-old.

None of us know yet how God plans to use our daughters. We don't know what battles He is currently equipping them for. A trait that seems like a flaw now may be a lifesaver down the road. There is no one "right" personality. While it is our job to teach, correct, and mold our daughters, we are ultimately called to respect their inherent design and help them become the best version of themselves.

3. Love her where she is.

Teenagers don't care what you know; they want to know that you care. Adults who talk down to them or expect them to listen without taking time to know them make teenagers tune out.

My daughter had a teacher who often complains about "kids these days." She fixates on how spoiled their generation is, and the students don't like her because she sees only the worst. She gives them no credit for what they do right, no hope for who they can be.

In contrast, my daughter had another teacher whom all the students love. As a middle school English instructor, he believes in teenagers at all levels of ability. When my friend's son struggled with the challenging curriculum, the teacher told him, "I'm not going to let you fail my class. You'll meet with me every Tuesday before school until we get your grade up." At an age when most kids feel overlooked, he notices and cares. He sends detailed emails to parents praising their child's progress and outlining areas of growth.

The Gospels are full of stories about Jesus meeting people where they are and accepting them regardless of their heart's condition. In stories like the woman at the well (John 4:1–42), where Jesus met a Samaritan woman who had been married five times and came to the well for water, we see His love and mercy in action.

Jesus told the woman that anyone who drinks from the well (pursues earthly pleasures) will always be thirsty, but those who accept His living water (the gift of eternal life) will never thirst again. The woman went back to town, leaving her jar behind, to tell others about this living water.

When I get impatient with my daughters, I try to think about how patient God is with me. I wonder how immature I must sound to someone ahead of me in their spiritual journey. I don't know what they know yet, but if they love me well, they'll inspire me to learn more.

Author Joanna Weaver says, "Jesus didn't come to make bad people better. He came to transform us into something entirely new."[4] God's kindness leads to repentance. Repentance leads to grace. Grace makes us new creations through Christ. By meeting your daughter where she is today, you give her a glimpse of her heavenly Father and the life-changing love that compels people to drop everything and follow Him.

4. Treat your daughter like she's already the person she's capable of becoming.

Our kids walk into the labels we give them. They live up to our expectations. If we want kind and strong kids, we must believe they have kindness and strength in them.

In the movie *The Help*, the character Aibileen Clark repeatedly tells the child she is raising, "You is smart, you is kind, you is important."[5] Why? Because she is casting a vision for how that little girl will see herself. She's clarifying her identity, and any choice or belief that contradicts that identity—like acting mean or calling herself dumb—isn't true to her character.

Your daughter is more capable than she believes. She was created for a purpose, to serve her generation like no one on the planet has ever served before. While God loves her exactly as she is today, He also has plans for her future—plans to cultivate Christlike character and shape her into His image.

Cast a vision for your daughter's life by helping her identify herself as a child of God. Let *that* be the label she walks into.

5. Remember your mess-ups.

My daughter took a beach trip with a friend and left her wallet in their condo. When she told me, my first thought was, *Really? How could she be so forgetful?* Her slipup annoyed me.

Later that day, God reminded me of a similar slipup. I had a speaking event in Little Rock, Arkansas, the year before, and in my rush to catch an early flight home, I left my hanging clothes in the hotel closet. Embarrassed, I had to call my host and ask if she'd mind retrieving my clothes and shipping them to me.

I often need a heart check to remember my girls are human just like me. I may be ahead of them in my life journey, but I'm also walking beside them as a sister in Christ.

Seeing your teenager's flaws is easy. Admitting your personal flaws takes humility. The older your daughter gets, the more necessary it is to remember we're all in the same boat—desperately in need of a Savior who loves us, even when we mess up.

6. Remember your influence.

As your daughter's mother, you hold remarkable power. Your view of her shapes her view of herself, because when a girl doesn't feel loved by her mother, she struggles to believe she is lovable.

Most moms love their daughters, and the disconnect often begins when our daughters act unloving toward us. When they push our buttons, talk back, give critical stares, or treat us like a dumping ground, the chasm opens.

One common instinct is to react—and bluntly set them straight. Ask any teen therapist what they hear in their office, and they'll share stories of moms harshly telling their daughters, "You're such a brat!" or "Why can't you be more like Sarah?" Words fly in the heat of the moment, and these rash reactions can derail relationships.

It is up to us as moms to act like grown-ups, to be tactful and separate what our daughters *do* from who they *are*. Rather than say, "You're a brat!" we can say, "That was a rude and hurtful remark, and you can't talk to me that way. If you do, you'll lose your phone." And should we lose our cool (which we all do at times!), we can apologize.

As the most influential female in your daughter's life, you have power, so use it for good. Remember how she longs for your approval. The people closest to us have the most power to hurt us, so when it's time to correct your daughter, do it in a spirit of love. Let her see what unconditional love looks like so she can extend it to herself and others.

7. Recognize the miracle in front of you.

When my girls were small, I dreaded adolescence. Every story I heard about teenage girls was negative, and the way most mothers put it, I was in for a dismal ride.

Because of this, I mourned their childhood. With every baby tooth they lost, every hair bow they refused to wear, every toy they stopped playing with, I wondered if we were leaving the peak experience of parenting, an age of innocence we'd never recapture.

I realized one day how this mentality was faulty. Instead of *mourning* my daughters' changes, I should *celebrate* them. Watching them grow up is a gift, and if I spend all my time looking back—dreaming about the little girls who once wore matching smocked dresses and sang Disney princess songs—I'll miss the beautiful scenes playing before me.

Honestly, I love my daughters more as teenagers than when

they were babies. While I certainly struggle more, I also connect with them on a deeper level. I love laughing with them, taking trips together, watching their personalities bloom, and marveling over who they are. As I enjoy this stage that we're in, I don't long for the past or wish to go back.

Your best days of parenting are *not* behind you. While the stress of adolescence can make any parent miss or romanticize the past, there is still great joy ahead. God is working in your daughter's life, and though this chapter may not look as magical as childhood, it is a special part of her story and yours.

8. Understand what's happening in her brain.

Your daughter may look like a grown-up and seem self-sufficient, but her brain is still developing.

Again, a teenager's brain is only 80 percent of the way to maturity. That 20 percent gap, according to neuroscientist Dr. Frances Jensen, is crucial and helps explain the puzzling behavior of teenagers, such as their mood swings, irritability, and impulsiveness; their inability to focus, to follow through, and to connect with adults; and their temptations to engage in risky behavior like drinking alcohol and using drugs.[6]

The teenage brain is in peak condition to learn and be influenced, yet Dr. Jensen compares it to a brand-new Ferrari that is primed and pumped but not yet road tested. It's all revved up—but unsure where to go.[7]

Teenagers are smart (smarter than adults in some ways), but expecting your daughter to think like a thirty-year-old is wishful thinking. Fortunately, she is still impressionable and hungry for guidance. Now is the time to invest in her life. Now is your chance to point her in a positive direction and say, "These are the strengths I see in you. . . . These are the gifts I believe will help you change the world."

Your daughter is listening, so seize the opportunity to impact her while her brain is still wiring and thus highly receptive to your feedback.

9. Know she is already criticizing herself.

After years of driving carloads of girls—and hearing private confessions from mothers—I can confirm that most girls doubt themselves. Even the most beautiful, popular, and talented ones you would never suspect.

Like grown women, girls tend to be tough on themselves. They may feel confident one minute and insecure the next as they take their eyes off their lane and compare themselves to the girls beside them.

With one glance, their confidence can plummet.

I believe most girls feel underappreciated and overlooked. Even if they're gorgeous and gifted, they're surrounded by gorgeous and gifted girls. They likely have someone in their circle who loves to tear them down, and their friends—as awesome as they may be—mostly think about themselves.

Words matter, and when someone's confidence is shaky, words matter even more. Even if your daughter acts like a tough cookie, it's safe to assume she has a fierce inner critic. She needs outside voices, especially yours, to help her be kind to herself.

10. Embrace grace.

Parents live in fear of teenagers hurting themselves. But what is equally scary is the thought of teenagers hating themselves. Many of us know what self-loathing feels like, and we're aware that we have an enemy who likes to lure us into temptation—and then makes us hate ourselves as regret or shame sets in.

Our world is unforgiving, especially to girls. A mistake that a girl makes in seventh grade can follow her for the rest of her life.

It can make her best friends ditch her and her classmates condemn her. Although God is merciful, forgiving every sin through Jesus, this isn't the reality teenagers see daily.

It's imperative for your daughter to know grace and understand how we all fall short of God's standard. Yet even at our worst, He loves us and desires a relationship. Your daughter's rock-bottom moments hold the most potential for her to understand grace because the love she receives when she feels alone and unworthy can turn her heart toward Him.

As author Anne Lamott says, "I do not at all understand the mystery of grace—only that it meets us where we are but does not leave us where it found us."[8]

Grace allows you to see your daughter through God's eyes and love her through her mistakes. It gives her the strength and courage to rise and try again. We all need more grace in our lives—and more people who give it freely.

The LORD said to Samuel, "Don't judge by his appearance or height, for I have rejected him. The LORD doesn't see things the way you see them. People judge by outward appearance, but the LORD looks at the heart."

–1 SAMUEL 16:7 NLT

YOUR DAUGHTER'S IDENTITY

I recently read that a girl's self-esteem peaks at nine years old.[9]

Sadly, that is *third grade.*

While I'm glad to hear that younger girls feel good about themselves, it breaks my heart that older girls do not.

What causes the shift? Many factors, but a big one is

self-consciousness. As girls grow up, they become keenly aware of (and concerned about) what other people think. They begin to tune in to cues and reactions, caring deeply about people's opinions of them.

And since relationships are important to girls, especially in the teen years, many girls will sacrifice what they really like—or who they really are—to fit in or belong.

That is why an academically gifted girl may want to take regular classes to be with her friends.

Why a fifth grader may stop playing with American Girl dolls because someone called her a baby.

Why middle schoolers dress like clones.

And why your daughter may delete old videos because she's embarrassed by how awkward and childish she used to be.

As your daughter hits adolescence, you may see her self-esteem shift. You may wonder:

How can I help her be confident in who she is?
How can I encourage authenticity?
Why does she worry so much about what people think?
Why does she exhaust herself chasing approval?
How can I teach her to think for herself?
Who is she trying to impress? Doesn't she know she has nothing to prove?

Girls often care more about what their *friends* think of them than what they think of *themselves*. They let the world tell them who to become and sometimes end up burying the best parts of themselves.

God designed your daughter (and you) to grow into His image. He wants her to live for His approval, not the world's approval, and find her identity in Christ.

How does she do that? By making Jesus her rock, the center of her universe. Overnight, she can lose everything the world tells her to base her identity on: beauty, talents, clothes, friends, boys, grades, material possessions, achievements, even her Instagram account. She can be stripped of every earthly trapping.

But what nobody can take away is her status as a child of God and the promise of heaven through Jesus. In Him, she has the hope of eternal life and a joy to cling to in all circumstances. Even if her worst nightmare came true, she'd still be standing with Christ as her foundation.

When discussing identity with your daughter, here are some things you can tell her.

- She is special because she exists—*period*. Nothing can make God love her more.
- She has inherent worth and dignity as God's child. What God creates, God loves. What God loves, He loves forever.
- The best part of her is God's Spirit inside her. The same Spirit that raised Jesus from the dead is what God gives to believers.
- She is meant to run her own race—to live authentically and not identically to anyone else.
- Her real identity is built from the inside out, beginning with letting Jesus into her heart.

Right now your daughter is figuring out who she is as an individual and as part of a group. She wants to be true to herself, yet she also wants to fit in.

Be patient as she wrestles, and remember how most of us build identities on what the world applauds us for. We often need a rude awakening to realize our mistake. Your daughter may have to lose the center of her universe—her closest friends, her boyfriend, her place on a team—to see how she built her identity on quicksand. She may struggle with insecurity before finding lasting security in Him.

What people say about your daughter is opinion, and what God says about her is fact. Help her find her identity in Christ and develop the armor she needs to live a life of courage, confidence, and purpose.

We are God's handiwork, created in Christ Jesus to do good works, which God prepared in advance for us to do.
—EPHESIANS 2:10

SELF-TALK AND SELF-IMAGE

Your daughter will hear a lot of voices in her life. While some voices will build her up, others will tear her down. What ultimately determines how she sees and feels about herself is the voice inside her head. Even if the world's applause is loud, a harsh inner critic will drown it out.

Maybe you can relate to this; I certainly can. Years ago, while getting ready for a date with my husband, I criticized myself in the mirror. Every flaw seemed to jump out, and I fixated on what looked wrong.

My husband heard me, and with great conviction he affirmed my beauty. I wouldn't listen because my mind stayed so focused on negative thoughts that his words barely registered.

He stared at me a long minute and grew quiet. With a saddened voice, he said, "I wish you could see yourself the way I see you. I don't know what else to say to convince you you're wrong."

His words hit hard because it felt like God was speaking to me. I wondered if He ever feels this way—saddened when we berate ourselves and refuse to see the good He made.

Your influence on your daughter is powerful yet limited. Even your best efforts to see the good in her won't guarantee results because you can't control her thoughts. Nobody ever "masters" self-love (just ask a grown woman!), but that's okay because struggles propel us toward Jesus. Struggles open our hearts to what God has to say.

God says remarkable things about your daughter and you. He has a vision for your lives that is unprecedented and unrevealed. Seeing your daughter or yourself correctly is never a perfect process, yet God's lens brings clarity. It counters lies with truth. On good days and bad ones, you and your daughter are wildly loved, embraced by a Father who sees your potential yet also accepts you exactly where you are.

"My sheep hear my voice, and I know them, and they follow me."

—JOHN 10:27 ESV

REFLECTION QUESTIONS

1. Describe yourself at age thirteen. Who loved you well (despite any awkwardness or rough edges) and cast a positive vision for your life?

2. When God looks at you, do you believe He sees a masterpiece with hidden potential? Why or why not?

3. How do your insecurities and personal baggage affect your view of your daughter? Do you ever treat her like your second chance or project your dreams and fears on her? Moving forward, how can you help her become who *she* is meant to be?

4. On a scale of one to ten, rate your daughter's self-esteem. When is she most confident and least confident? What does she base her identity on?

5. On a scale of one to ten, rate your self-esteem. When are you most confident and least confident? What do you base your identity on?

6. How do you think God sees your daughter? What can you learn from Him?

. . . .

· 6 · · · · · · · · · · · · · · · ·

HELP HER FIND GOOD FRIENDS AND POSITIVE INFLUENCES

I can't overstate the significance of a
teenager's tribe membership. Teenagers
aren't just looking to make friends,
they are replacing the family they've
withdrawn from (or, at least, might barely
acknowledge in public) with a tribe that
they can feel proud to call their own.
—DR. LISA DAMOUR[1]

What makes or breaks a girl's high school experience," a woman in youth ministry once told me, "is her friendships."

She knows from experience. While her oldest daughter had terrific friendships and loved high school, her second daughter had tumultuous friendships and hated high school. She couldn't graduate fast enough.

This woman had an accurate word to describe female friendships during the teenage years: *fluid*.

Friendships change a lot in adolescence, ebbing and flowing as girls explore new friendships and sometimes grow apart. As girls' passions, personalities, and circumstances evolve, their relationships evolve too.

For moms, this fluidity is hard to watch, and here are some reasons why:

1. We get attached to certain friends—and their mothers—and we want the bonds to last forever.
2. We see the pain behind the scenes as our daughters come home, burst into tears, and share hurtful events.
3. We see our daughters deflate as they scroll through social media and realize they were left out.
4. We feel helpless trying to help them, even if our mother-daughter relationship is strong, because our company is no substitute for real friends.
5. We want security in our daughters' friendships because we know how influential friends are and we're aware of the challenges ahead that friends should weather together.

I hear so many stories about the friendship struggles that today's girls face. Technology has thrown teenagers for a major loop, and as digital interactions replace face-to-face encounters, it has become easier than ever to hurt feelings, ruin relationships, and harm reputations.

For teenage girls, friends are like oxygen. Your daughter needs friends for the same reasons you need friends: they make life better. They "get" her in a special way. They cushion pain and trigger laughter. They create a magical world that lets her escape and forget her worries for a while.

As we all know, however, not all friends are equal. Not all friendships go the distance and last twenty years or more. One way to connect with your daughter is to be her rock as she navigates friendships, to offer sound and solid guidance on how to make friends, keep friends, and—most importantly—become the friend she hopes to find.

———————— • ————————

There are "friends" who destroy each other, but a real friend sticks closer than a brother.

—PROVERBS 18:24 NLT

———————— • ————————

TIMELESS TRUTHS OF FRIENDSHIP

My friend tells her nine-year-old daughter that building good relationships is the hardest thing she'll do in life.

It's also the most *important* thing her daughter will do in life. According to the longest study on happiness, conducted by Harvard researchers, close relationships—more than money or fame—keep people happy throughout their lives.

"The surprising finding is that our relationships and how happy we are in our relationships has a powerful influence on our health," says Robert Waldinger, a professor of psychiatry at Harvard Medical School. "Taking care of your body is important, but tending to your relationships is a form of self-care too. That, I think, is the revelation."

Experiencing loneliness is toxic, Waldinger adds, and people can feel lonely even in relationships and crowds.[2]

Clearly, warm relationships matter. So how do you empower your daughter to build a thriving network? How do you help her invest her time wisely—and in the *right* relationships?

There is no magic bullet, but there are guidelines for healthy friendships that stand the test of time. Here are some to share with your daughter.

Twenty Truths of Friendship

1. A good friend will draw you closer to the people who love you most, like family and close friends.

Anyone who distances your daughter from loved ones, stirs up tension in long-standing relationships, or tries to isolate, control, or manipulate her so she listens only to them is a person to avoid.

2. The closer you are to God, the better friend you'll be.

Since God is love, we all need God in our heart to show love. The traits of a good friend—love, joy, peace, kindness, goodness, faithfulness, gentleness, patience, and self-control—come through the fruit of the Holy Spirit. Humans are drawn to love and warmth, and the source of both is God.

3. The perfect friend doesn't exist.

Expecting friends to be perfect is unfair because only Jesus is the perfect friend. The rest of us are human. We get moody, make mistakes, and disappoint our loved ones.

No one friend can meet all your daughter's needs, so remind your daughter to appreciate a girl's strengths while accepting her limitations (and remember how she has strengths and limitations too). While some friends will make your daughter laugh, other friends will make her think. While some friends will plan her birthday party, other friends will *be* the party. And while some friends will keep her secrets, other friends will scream from a rooftop to cheer her on.

Having a variety of friends takes the pressure off any one person to be your daughter's be-all and end-all. It makes your daughter a good friend because she isn't impossible to please.

4. Friends aren't meant to be worshiped.

God created us to worship Him, but sometimes we worship idols. We take a good thing—like friendship—and make it the ultimate thing, revolving our life around it.

When your daughter makes friends the center of her universe, it sets the stage for disappointment. Friends are amazing, but they're not her Savior. They have their own issues, and they aren't meant to solve all your daughter's problems, eliminate all her pain, or always be available. A great friendship keeps God at the center. It lets your daughter experience His love through tangible connections.

5. Exclusive friend groups are unhealthy.

A girl told her mother that by the time she graduated, she had a friend in every friend group. This is healthy. What isn't healthy are friend groups that get so tight nobody notices, associates with, or talks to anyone beyond the group.

Friend groups with absolute borders operate like gangs. No one gets in, no one gets out, and anyone who breaks a rule is ostracized. It's a microcosm of the power play seen at every level of society. At many schools, friend groups get so solidified that girls stay in groups they've outgrown, even when they're miserable. They're afraid that if they do leave, no group will take them in.

Fear is never a good reason to stay in a relationship, and your daughter will never reach her potential surrounded by the wrong people. Even if she has to start over, rebuilding her network one friend at a time, she'll have hope. It's okay to have a friend group, but make sure the girls who influence your daughter give her room to grow and continue making new friendships.

6. Forced friendships never work.

Just as your daughter can't force a boy to fall in love with her, she can't force a girl to like her. And why try? Why waste her time trying to win over a girl who could take her or leave her when there are real friends to pursue?

Your daughter doesn't want to look back twenty years from now and realize she poured her heart and soul into relationships that didn't build her up. Forced friendships always expire, so encourage your daughter to find friends who love her back and reciprocate her efforts rather than chasing a girl to win her approval.

7. You won't thrive in every environment, and that's okay.

You daughter won't always fit in or belong. She may have countless friends in middle school yet no friends she can count on in high school. She may be in heaven during English class yet bored out of her mind in biology. She may feel appreciated at one party yet totally ignored at another.

Everyone wants easy rapport, instant connections, and common passions, but that magic can be elusive. Help your daughter set realistic expectations and know that some seasons and groups will be tough. Some dynamics and environments will better match her personality and strengths. Rather than doubt herself when she feels out of place, she can make the best of these situations by continuing to meet new people and look for common ground.

8. You won't click with everyone, and that's okay too.

That's life. But encourage your daughter to be friendly and stay open to future friendships. People change, mature, and grow up. People will also come back into her life.

A girl whom your daughter doesn't click with now may become a good friend later, possibly decades down the road as they end up at the same law school or their kids fall in love or their husbands meet through work. You never know how God will later weave two stories together, so teach your daughter to look for the good in people, keep a friendly rapport, and avoid burning bridges.

9. Friendship should be a source of comfort, not stress.

Your daughter is surrounded by pessimists and critics. The last thing she needs is friends who add to this negativity by dissing her, using her, excluding her, targeting her as the punch line of jokes, or making her feel bad about herself.

True friends are honest yet compassionate. They may disagree with your daughter, challenge her, or express concern over a bad choice, but it's because they care. They don't want your daughter to settle for less than she deserves. Above all, they love her and want her to succeed.

10. Nothing kills friendships quicker than jealousy and comparison.

Your daughter may feel confident one minute—and then insecure the next as she compares herself to the girl beside her. Yet

God created her to run *her* race in *her* lane. No girl must lose her race so that your daughter can win hers.

Friendships fail when girls secretly hope for their friends to fail. We all get jealous and resentful at times, but rather than dwell on these feelings, remind your daughter to pray for help. Remind her that when she feels jealous, she can do the opposite of how she feels and *compliment* her friend on the very thing she envies. With time, her actions can alter her feelings.

What is good for one girl is good for all girls. A win for one is a win for all. Our world loves to pit girls against each other and make us believe that every girl is out for herself, but that's not true. Don't let a few bad apples ruin your daughter's faith in females. At every age, it is possible to find genuine friends who cheer each other on.

11. Love your friends well and be loyal, but keep a loose grip.

It is good for your daughter to give her friends space to explore new friendships. It is also good for her to explore new friendships herself.

Your daughter can never make too many friends. Making friends wherever she goes will enrich her life, grow her heart, and expand her thinking. It increases the odds that she'll have someone making choices similar to her choices, even if her best friends do not. Most importantly, it lets your daughter show love to a wider and more diverse circle.

12. Form your own opinions about people, and don't believe everything you hear.

Just because your daughter's friend dislikes someone doesn't mean she should too. Just because a rumor is flying around doesn't mean it is true. Help your daughter treat everyone like a friend until they give her a good reason not to, and, when possible, give people the benefit of the doubt.

13. There is a difference between committed friends and casual friends.

Committed friends are the ones your daughter will carry through life. They have her back and will stand in her corner as her last friends standing.

Casual friends are the ones she'll have for a season of life, maybe a few seasons. They'll have fun together and their personalities will click, but there won't be a great deal of loyalty or longevity in these relationships.

Committed friends will make up a *small* portion of your daughter's social network. Casual friends will make up a *large* part. Committed friends can typically be counted on one hand, and if your daughter has that, she's lucky.

14. While you are called to love everyone, not everyone deserves a place in your innermost circle.

Not everybody is meant to be your BFF.

Some people your daughter can love up close and personal because they're trustworthy and good for her. Other people she needs to love at an arm's length because inviting them into her life can breed disaster. She can be kind and wish them well, but she doesn't need to tell them her deepest, darkest secrets or ask them to spend the night.

Your daughter's closest friends should lift her up, have strong values, and encourage her to become her best self. They should be her armor against the pain of this world and have her best interests in mind.

15. Your loneliest seasons of friendship will produce your best lessons in friendship.

Being an outsider will help your daughter realize that true friends are a gift.

Being new in town, having no friends, or having a friend group unexpectedly turn on her will teach your daughter empathy and compassion. It will help her realize what a kind word, a smile, or an invitation to a party can mean to a girl who hasn't found her people yet—or who has lost her people completely.

This awareness may lead your daughter to suddenly notice people who sit alone and invite them to join her. It may help her push past shyness and anxiety to make new friends rather than waiting for other girls to make the first move. It may inspire her to be proactive, initiate conversations, and show genuine interest in others.

It is painful to watch your daughter face a lonely season of friendship, but these seasons can take her friendship game up another notch. Through pain, she can learn to be kinder, more inclusive, and more outgoing. And when she does find her people, she'll be less likely to take them for granted.

16. Casting a wide net—and being kind to everyone—keeps your friend options open.

Girls often paint themselves into a corner by being friendly only to a select group. They get so cozy with their inner circle that they never branch out, and they miss opportunities to make new friends and build a diverse social network.

Encourage your daughter to cast a wide net and make friends wherever she goes: PE class, driver's ed, tumbling lessons, summer camp, church, or an out-of-town birthday party. Besides making her life more interesting, this expanded network will teach her how kindness builds bridges and is good for the heart.

Should her core friends let her down, she'll have other friends to turn to. These extra sources of comfort could be her saving grace during a hard season.

17. Bad company ruins good morals.

A high school principal told his children, "It only takes one bad apple to spoil the bunch." He'd seen firsthand how much damage one person can do to change a group or class dynamic.

It's important for your daughter to choose good company. If she thinks she can hang around a wilder crowd and lift them up to her standards, she's wrong. Instead, they'll pressure her to lower her standards. Sooner or later a bad influence rubs off, and your daughter will either make choices against her better judgment or wind up in a predicament.

A mom I know told her daughter about a high school crush who was very sweet to her yet also wild. She didn't see the issue until they had their first date—and he took her to a drug dealer's house. She told her daughter, "Even though I was innocent, I would have gone to jail if the police had come. I was guilty by association just by being there."

There's an old saying that is particularly relevant to teen friendships: "Show me your friends, and I'll show you your future." Friend choices matter, and just as your daughter should set standards for herself, she should also set standards for her closest friends.

18. The worst thing to do when you feel lonely is dwell in loneliness.

The best thing your daughter can do when she feels lonely is (1) talk to someone trustworthy or (2) look around, see who else looks lonely, and reach out.

All around your daughter every day, peers are struggling

with loneliness. They're craving real connection and searching for one true friend. They may be surrounded by people yet still feel lonely if their relationships lack intimacy.

God created your daughter for community, and the way to survive a lonely spell is by looking outward and connecting with people who keep her from isolating herself.

19. Some girls act mean.

Some girls stir the pot. Some girls expect blind obedience. Your daughter will be much happier if she avoids this negativity.

There is a lot of misery in friendships today due to poor friend choices. Just as your daughter can't make negative choices and expect a positive life, she can't choose selfish friends and expect uplifting relationships.

Dr. Lisa Damour offers insight into why girls choose this route.

> Research suggests that girls who bully other girls often do so to create a sense of belonging or to alleviate boredom in their group by creating excitement. In other words, girls sometimes find their place in a tribe by harassing or excluding girls who don't fit with the group norms. They may also target their peers to create social "glue"—something to talk about, something to do—when they lack the maturity to come together around positive interests. [3]

Yes, friends should laugh and have fun, but *what* your daughter and her friends laugh about and bond over matters. Friendships that center around gossip, making fun of people, starting rumors, hating people, and blind obedience aren't real friendships.

Negativity will affect your daughter's spirit and health. She can kindly distance herself, keep her guard up, and use bad experiences to remember who she doesn't want to be.

20. The best friends act as encouragers, not competitors.

A competitive spirit may work on a playing field, but in relationships, it does damage.

As Dr. Meg Meeker says, "Many times girls gain a sense of superiority over their peers when they excel at something. And when this happens, they can become isolated from friends, peers, and family. Competitiveness creeps in. Their sense of superiority makes their world small and self-contained. They find no joy in what's around them. They focus on success, not on friends."[4]

Nobody wants an ultra-competitive friend. Nobody needs a friend who only thinks of herself. Real friendship grows when two girls champion each other—encouraging each other's dreams, pointing out each other's talents, and celebrating each other out loud.

Friendships like this require confidence and maturity, two girls secure enough in who they are to look beyond their self-interests.

Your daughter's friendships will ebb and flow, but in all circumstances, she has security in God. Even on bad days, when she feels rejected or lost, He loves her deeply.

This truth is a lifeline. It's a hope to cling to when your daughter is crying, scared, or worried. It may take a friendship rift for her to realize why she needs Jesus, why He's the only reliable anchor when a storm hits, and if that is her biggest takeaway from a relationship heartache, consider it a gift. God never wastes pain, and even the pain of friendship can present new opportunities for your daughter to grow in faith.

The LORD is near to all who call on him, to all who call on him in truth.

—PSALM 145:18

PLEASE DON'T TELL YOUR DAUGHTER "GIRLS ARE MEAN"

We've all been there, right? Even if you didn't verbalize it, you may have felt tempted to repeat the cliché.

Girls are mean.

Typically, it happens after your daughter gets hurt, after another girl's words or actions have cut her to the core. Desperate to comfort her and at a loss for words, you may reach for the low-hanging fruit, the first words that come to mind because society constantly repeats them.

But let me ask you: Do you believe it? Do you agree *all* girls are mean? If so, you're saying you are mean, your daughter is mean, and there is no hope for any of us. What good does that serve, and what hope for friendship will our daughters ever have if we teach them to be skeptical of all girls and expect the worst?

We find what we're looking for in life, and when we buy into blanket statements, they become self-fulfilling prophecies.

In my opinion, girls don't have a monopoly on being mean. Boys can be cruel as well, and what we have is not a gender issue but a cultural issue—a society that's grown incredibly heartless.

I'm sure my daughters will have issues one day due to my

maternal missteps, but one issue I don't want them struggling to reverse is a deep distrust of girls. They need good friends, and for every girl who acts mean, there are five others who do not.

When another girl hurts your daughter, instill hope and a sense of control. Consider a script like this to replace the "girls are mean" stereotype that is never across-the-board true:

I'm so sorry this happened. It's not right or fair, and you don't deserve it. Please know you're not alone. Although you feel singled out, like you're the only person in the universe to be treated this way, you're not.

Sadly, our world sets a low bar for how people should behave. Even at my age, people can be mean, ugly, and inconsiderate. Just last week someone hurt my feelings with a rude remark. I can't promise you'll never be hurt again, but you can use this situation to your advantage. It can make you a better friend.

The worst behaviors provide the best examples of how not to act. Now that you've been the target of mean behavior, you know never to repeat it. This wisdom and empathy will take you far in life and lead to great relationships.

This may blow over or it may not. Only time will tell. For now, keep a safe distance from this person and stick with people who make you feel good. Take the high road because it keeps you at peace with yourself and attracts true friends.

You can't "fix" anyone or make them stop being mean, but you can stop the hate. Let's go for kind and be the example our world needs. Help other girls whom you see struggling, and be the friend you wish you had right now.

The scripts we hand our daughters wire them for relationships. They tell them what to look for and what to expect.

Together we can improve the conversation. We can avoid clichés and empower our daughters—even in hurtful times—to be proud of their gender and optimistic for what's to come.

"Yes, just as you can identify a tree by its fruit, so you can identify people by their actions."

–MATTHEW 7:20 NLT

TEEN FRIENDSHIPS: THEY MATTER

Someone once said, "If you want to know your child, look at their friends," and it's true. You can learn a lot about your daughter by getting to know her friends and who she is drawn to.

As your daughter pulls away from you, she'll gravitate toward friends. By her senior year of high school, her friends will play a pivotal role in shaping who she becomes and what direction her life takes. My college roommate and I often talk about how we helped each other grow up. We both made many mistakes, but we loved each other through them and had each other's backs.

For my daughters and yours, I want friends who have their backs. Friends who point them in the right direction and ultimately feel like family, their home away from home.

Even if you and your daughter have been burned by friends, remember there are kind girls and kind women out there who are hungry for love, connection, and belonging. They long for loyalty, and their hearts are open. It's worth taking a chance on each other.

In every season, there are opportunities for you and your daughter to make new friends. Friendships begin when someone takes the first step, so let's raise girls who do that. Let's help them be brave and confident in putting themselves out there and noticing girls who are ready and willing to build real friendships.

———————— • ————————

Let us consider how we may spur one another on toward love and good deeds, not giving up meeting together, as some are in the habit of doing, but encouraging one another—and all the more as you see the Day approaching.

–HEBREWS 10:24–25

———————— • ————————

REFLECTION QUESTIONS

. . . .

1. Why do so many girls today struggle with friendships? How can moms help without getting overly involved?

2. Describe a time when you and your daughter navigated a tricky friend issue. What did you learn? What did she learn?

3. Are adult friendships "fluid" like teen friendships? Why or why not?

4. Have you ever told your daughter "girls are mean"? Has your daughter told you this? What do you think of this statement?

5. What is your go-to friendship advice when your daughter is feeling down?

6. Name a friend who was in your daughter's life for only a season yet left a positive impact. What do friendships like this—that are short-lived and come when we need them—teach us?

BE HER EMOTIONAL COACH

Girls, more than ever, are in need of
emotional support from their parents
because they are not getting it where they
are spending most of their time: online.
–LISBETH SPLAWN[1]

Afriend called me about an issue I often get asked about.
As a mom of younger girls, she is facing what I have gone
through with three of my four daughters.

"My daughter's always been so sweet," she said. "But lately
she's been different. She gets mad over the smallest things, and I
don't know what I've done."

I assured her that her daughter is normal. I also understood
her exasperation and unspoken fears.

Right when mothers desire a close relationship, we feel our
daughters pull away. Our once comfortable connection feels

unsteady or jeopardized. Some days our daughters like us—and some days we're not sure. At times we feel like the enemy as they forget we're on their side.

A mother knows when the winds start to change, and though the timing was different for each of my daughters, the common thread was heightened moodiness, defensiveness, and irritability. More attitude than normal and sporadic edginess.

My biggest mistake, which took time for me to recognize and correct, was mirroring my daughter's reaction. If she got angry, I did too. If she snapped, I snapped back. This deepened the wedge between us and shut her down. It was also immature of me.

By focusing on my emotions and how my daughter made *me* feel, I failed to provide the emotional support and role model she needed. I became so sensitive to her pushback and withdrawal that I dismissed the inner turmoil that could explain her new behavior.

Now I remind myself that adolescence is hard. It's an unpredictable season that throws teenagers into the perfect storm of puberty, self-consciousness, self-doubt, comparison, social and academic pressures, and a flood of changes in their bodies, moods, friendships, and circumstances.

For the first time, girls are having *big* thoughts, *big* feelings, and *big* emotions. They're unsure how to deal with them, so they may unleash on Mom or anyone who feels safe because of unconditional love.

Adolescence presents a huge opportunity to reconnect with your daughter as her emotional coach. Even as she pulls away, she needs your help to process life and sort through the blizzard stirring inside her.

A psychologist once told me that the part of the brain that interprets emotions is developmentally behind the emotions themselves. When teenagers feel angry or sad, they can't always figure out why. Even a little clarity, discernment, or timely wisdom can boost their ability to cope.

As my daughters grow up, they need me more emotionally, yet I often miss the mark. I may try three wrong approaches before finding one that really clicks. If you hit a wall, don't give up. Your daughter needs you, and finding an approach that keeps her talking and coming to you is worth the effort it takes.

"I am leaving you with a gift—peace of mind and of heart. And the peace I give you is a gift the world cannot give. So don't be troubled or afraid."

—JOHN 14:27 NLT

LET HER HAVE FEELINGS

"You and Dad are always like, *perspective*," my daughter once said, "but I'm allowed to be upset over dumb things for five minutes."

"You're right," I replied. "And I need to keep that in mind."

The truth is, I can be impatient. I've been guilty of rushing my daughters through unpleasant feelings by giving pep talks or life lessons. I've told my daughters how they *should* feel before listening to how they *do* feel. I've expected them to master emotions that still elude me at times.

What they need first, I have found, is space. Space to vent. Space to unload. Space to say or acknowledge what they might never say to someone's face or post online but will feel much better about once they voice it out loud.

I have one daughter who has realized that after a good cry

she always feels better. She's learned how cathartic crying can be, so she lets herself go there. While my instinct is to "fix" emotions that make me uncomfortable—or make *me* want to cry—my girls benefit more when I let them feel and face their emotions. After all, emotions buried alive always resurface.

As moms, we help our daughters when we do these things:

- Listen empathetically.
- Let them talk freely.
- Stay calm and remain a voice of reason.
- Give words to their thoughts and emotions.
- Avoid mirroring their reactions.
- Stay calm, strong, and centered, not letting our mood revolve around their mood or putting pressure on them to be strong for *us*.
- Assure them that their feelings are normal.
- Help them find healthy outlets (such as art, music, exercise, journaling, Scripture).
- Teach them mature ways to work through and think through anger, sadness, resentment, disappointment, frustration, and stress.
- Help them see the next step.

Dr. Lisa Damour says teenagers often have the right feeling on the wrong scale. We can bring their feelings down to size by giving a name to them, talking about them, and using a tone that conveys warmth and total confidence that our daughters will bounce back. Not making a team, for instance, could be met with this response: "I know how much you wanted to be on varsity and that you are really disappointed. The outcome hurts."[2]

I know a family with five teenagers who talks a lot about recovery. They listen to their kids' struggles, and when the time is right, the dad asks, "What will your recovery be? How will you respond to this setback?" I like this statement because it gives our daughters a solid track to run on. Once they identify their emotions and feel them, they can think about how to channel them in healthy, productive ways.

God is not a God of disorder but of peace—as in all the congregations of the Lord's people.

—1 CORINTHIANS 14:33

TEACH HER EMOTIONAL SELF-CONTROL

You've probably met girls who act like bulls in a china shop.

Maybe you've *been* that bull in a china shop, creating relationship wreckage as your emotions spun out of control.

Either way, you've seen firsthand how unbridled feelings can create havoc. Feelings are great followers—yet terrible leaders. Just because we feel emotions doesn't give us the right to act on them. Some days I may feel like clawing somebody's eyes out. Some days I'm irritable and sensitive. Some days I'm annoyed by everyone through no fault of their own.

One perk of getting older is that we know ourselves and can recognize our triggers. We see the warning signs that precede an outburst or meltdown, and we can respond accordingly (giving ourselves space, taking a walk, praying, etc.). Our daughters, on the other hand, are still learning. They're still getting acquainted with their moods and triggers.

It is impossible to have healthy relationships without emotional intelligence. Emotional intelligence is your daughter's ability to understand and regulate her emotions while understanding and reading the emotions of others—and letting that knowledge influence her words, choices, and behavior.

An emotionally intelligent girl knows not to send angry texts when she's seeing red. She can tune in to her feelings without dumping them on others. She empathizes with friends who are down and need encouragement. She listens to her instincts and intuition. She pays attention to body language and facial cues. She finds healthy outlets for her pain. She works on these learned behaviors.

We all want emotionally intelligent friends, but to attract friends like that, we must get ourselves in a good place first. Here are ideas to help your daughter reach that goal.

Fifteen Ways to Be Your Daughter's Emotional Coach

1. Remember that a teenager's response to the world is driven by emotion, not reason.

Dr. Frances Jensen says that during adolescence, more than any other time, emotions rule our lives. The main difference between adults and adolescents is much less activity in the frontal lobes of adolescents, making it harder for them to handle their emotions, especially in a crisis.

"Teenagers are usually up or they're down," she explains, "and they are very rarely something in between. As parents we sometimes experience our teenagers' emotional highs and lows as frighteningly out of control, and because our teenagers are as of yet unable to smooth things out using their frontal lobes, it's up to us to be the filter, the regulator, to provide the sense of calm their brains can't yet provide."[3]

Teenagers have a hyperactive amygdala (the primitive part of the brain, the center of the "fight or flight" instinct) and an underdeveloped prefrontal cortex (the rational part of brain that doesn't fully develop until age twenty-five or so). This gap helps explain the heightened emotions that distort reality. By acting as your daughter's reality check, you can be a voice of reason and calm in the chaos.

2. Love your daughter and let her vent— but don't be her punching bag.

Teenagers push limits, and sometimes we moms take more than we should. Why? Because we sympathize with their struggles. We don't feel like fighting. We're scared of losing them. We know they're stressed, so we let them cross certain lines.

But if you tolerate disrespect, you set a bad precedent. One day it won't be you who your daughter is coming home to; it will be her *roommate*, her *spouse*, her *child*. It's okay for your daughter to vent and unload, but not if she disrespects you or someone else in the process.

I've had to tell all my girls, "You can't talk to me like that. I love you, but I won't let you disrespect me. If you do, you'll lose privileges." Setting a standard of respect is an act of love that will help your daughter have healthy relationships and keep her emotions in check.

3. Watch for rumination.

It's good for girls to talk about their problems, but dwelling on them is another story. There comes a point where enough is enough, and it's time to move on. In today's culture of self-focus, girls often get so wrapped up in their feelings that they ignore the feelings of those around them, and that is one reason why we see so much loneliness and depression. One cure for this is service or an act of kindness, helping your daughter get out of her head, forget about herself, and think about someone else.

4. Encourage self-care.

Controlling emotions is easier when your daughter is in fighting condition. When her life is a flurry of too much stress, too little sleep, poor eating habits, and an overload of screen time, her defenses come down. She becomes vulnerable and likely to snap. Feeling rested and healthy can make a big difference in how she responds to her day.

5. Help her avoid technology when she's not feeling the love.

We all get angry and overreact at times, but keeping these moments private—and undocumented—can prevent your daughter from burning bridges. People don't forget the accusations, attacks, or passive-aggressive remarks that fly in heated moments, so remind your daughter to stay off technology until she has cooled down. Otherwise, she may ruin a relationship by channeling her emotions into a keypad.

6. Let her sit with her anxiety.

My friend's daughter struggled with anxiety before high school started. Like most moms, she reassured her daughter that fears like getting locked into a locker wouldn't happen—until a psychologist told her to let her daughter sit with her anxiety.

Rather than say, "That won't happen, sweetie," she began asking, "Do you really think that might happen? Is that a rational thought?" Initially it was hard for this mom to see her daughter wrestle with her own thoughts, but with the counselor's help, this girl learned to calm herself down and started to create art as a healthy outlet.

When teenagers don't learn to sit with their anxiety, it can be a breeding ground for addiction as they look to shortcuts (like alcohol) to deal with stress. Sometimes a simple coping mechanism equips them to help themselves.

7. Teach her to resolve peer conflict.

When another girl hurts your daughter, should you get involved?

Here's an easy answer: ask your daughter.

Nine times out of ten, she won't want you to step in. She knows the tension will get worse if you call the other girl's mom.

Why? Because things can turn ugly when mama bear gets involved. Your daughter may pay the price through social isolation. There are two sides to every story, and you hear only one. Other mothers love their daughters as much as you love yours, and as much as you'd like to fix the mean girls, you can't fight your daughter's battles. She needs to learn how to handle hurtful people, and under your instruction, she can.

Sometimes intervention is necessary, especially when safety is at risk. But save your phone calls for the big incidents so you don't become known as "that mom." Oftentimes what your daughter needs most is someone who will listen, empathize, and brainstorm options of what to do next.

8. Encourage one-on-one resolution.

Most girls never learn conflict resolution. When they feel hurt or upset, they blow up or bottle it up. They give the offender a piece of their mind, or they pretend they're fine while letting the truth seep out through underhanded jabs, cold shoulders, and passive-aggressive remarks.

What starts as a conflict between two *girls* often escalates into an issue between two *groups* as word spreads and people take sides. A girl gets her feelings hurt, and rather than talk with the person who hurt her, she talks it out with everyone *but* that person.

This breeds drama. This blows issues out of proportion. This provokes everyone, turning friend groups into gangs.

Issues can often be resolved (or partially settled) when two girls talk without accusations. When one can calmly say, "Hey, this wasn't like you, but it really hurt my feelings when you kept teasing me at lunch. I don't want this to come between us, and that's why I'm telling you, because I value our friendship and want to work through it."

This approach makes a friend more likely to listen and less likely to get defensive. It gives her a chance to apologize and keeps little issues from turning into big ones.

9. Limit her social media time.

I've yet to see a study that says spending time online makes girls feel better about themselves.

What I do see is massive evidence of the negative side effects of social media and screen time. As Lisbeth Splawn wrote on Dr. Meg Meeker's website, "For teen girls today, the greatest obstacle to emotional health is social media."[4]

As we all know, many girls are addicted. They cling to their phones like life support. Only with intervention will they take necessary breaks. You know your daughter better than anyone, and you care more about her well-being than anyone, so don't hesitate to set boundaries when you think she needs them.

10. Talk about empathy.

I once heard a therapist say, "We live in a culture where kids are losing awareness that there are two sides to a story."

Sadly, our parenting culture is largely to blame because when we treat our kids as the center of the universe, they fail to learn empathy.

Empathy is the ability to understand someone else's thoughts, feelings, and point of view. Even if your daughter isn't naturally empathetic, she can learn empathy through practice, by getting in the mental habit of stepping into someone else's shoes and contemplating what life might be like for that person.

Last summer the contractor who was redoing our driveway fell behind schedule. I was frustrated, but as I saw him working alone one day because his employees didn't show up, sweat dripping down his face in the hot Alabama sun, my heart softened. Rather than get mad, I got him lunch and a huge drink. He later told my husband how much he appreciated the meal because he hadn't eaten all day. We learned that his wife had cancer and he had other burdens as well, and I was so glad that I'd refrained from acting on my emotions.

Every day presents opportunities for you and your daughter to discuss and practice empathy. Even in conflict, even when someone else is clearly wrong, you can show the kind of empathy that builds bridges, diffuses anger, and works toward peaceful resolutions.

11. Help her cultivate a healthy thought life.

Your daughter gets to choose the way she thinks. She gets to choose her attitude too. More important than any conversation you have with her is the conversation she has with herself. Is it negative? Prideful? Preoccupied with appearance? Does her mind spin out of control with worries, fears, and lies from the enemy that impact her perception and treatment of others? Through Christ, God can renew her mind and help her create a healthy thought life that gives birth to healthy choices, actions, and habits.

12. Empower her to handle hurtful people.

Your daughter is a flawed, imperfect human surrounded by flawed, imperfect humans. She will never stop encountering hurtful people, but she can learn to deal with them.

How? By understanding that nobody is a waste. Everyone serves a purpose. The worst behaviors offer the best examples of how *not* to act, and while some people teach her who she does want to be, others teach her who she doesn't want to be. Even sharks can offer unforgettable lessons on social graces, dignity, and the importance of being kind.

Many people become kind after they are hurt because they promise themselves never to make anyone else feel the same way. They boost their emotional IQ by letting their pain become their teacher. Your daughter can't control how other people treat her, but she can control her response. She can do the right thing and save her energy for positive people, choosing a path that God can (and will) bless.

13. Set a good example.

A psychologist once told me, "I never respond to my first reaction." Why? Because knee-jerk reactions are rarely the best course of action, especially when emotions run high.

Your daughter is watching you, and your response to events impacts her response to events. Whatever you expect of her, practice it in your life too. Show her how it looks to have measured responses.

14. See conflicts as opportunities.

Emotional intelligence grows best in loving relationships, especially when differences arise.

Your daughter may not realize that not everyone thinks like her until her blunt honesty makes a sensitive friend cry. If she holds grudges, she may not value grace until a friend forgives her and then moves on. Through conflict, your daughter gets exposed to different viewpoints, and as she learns from them, she will expand her heart, mind, and network. She will begin to understand more people and become less apt to make assumptions or judge.

15. Remind her to get quiet with God.

When your daughter feels emotional, she may want to immediately call a friend or talk to you. This isn't wrong, but sometimes the best place to go is straight to God. He is the author of peace, not confusion, and by making a habit of talking to Him, she can discover the peace that surpasses all understanding.

We moms can take our daughters only as far as we have come. To be an emotional coach, we must be emotionally healthy ourselves, always growing our intelligence and seeking professional help when our daughters need more than we can provide.

———————— • ————————

If any of you lacks wisdom, you should ask God, who gives generously to all without finding fault, and it will be given to you.

—JAMES 1:5

———————— • ————————

HEALTHY EMOTIONS, HEALTHY LIFE

I once fell apart because our family lost a home we thought was a done deal.

The owners told us their house was ours and set a closing date. Then they used our contract to get a higher offer. We learned about their deceit as we were celebrating our new home at dinner.

I cried all weekend and felt all the feelings. I'd gotten attached to this home, and so had my children, because after years of living in close quarters, we were finally getting more space. I needed to unleash, and for lack of a better option, I threw shoes at my bedroom wall.

I was a few sneakers and stilettos in when my nine-year-old

daughter wandered into the room. She looked confused at first, but as I explained the method to my madness, she joined me in throwing shoes. Slowly, my anger stirred her anger, and for a minute we both felt better dinging the sheetrock for revenge.

But then it hit me what I had done. My mood had shaped her mood. My frustration had stoked her frustration. I was influencing her emotions, and while I wanted her to be honest about her disappointment, I couldn't leave her in this volatile place. I decided in that moment to harness my anger and contain the monster in me.

We all have a monster that gets provoked by difficult people and dashed expectations. While it's okay to channel raw emotions into safe physical outlets (like a punching bag), we also need strategies to take our emotions to a more evolved place.

Your daughter's emotions can make her or break her. They will affect every relationship she has, down to her children and grandchildren. Coaching her now, while she is primed to learn, can reap big-time dividends. It can tip the scales in helping her become her best self possible.

Your daughter is smart, and she can take a good word and run with it. Train her to handle her emotions, and you'll point her toward a lifetime of peace and strong relationships.

———————— • ————————

Let the peace of Christ rule in your hearts, since as members of one body you were called to peace. And be thankful.

–COLOSSIANS 3:15

———————— • ————————

REFLECTION QUESTIONS

1. When did your daughter's emotions intensify? How did that shift impact your relationship?

2. When your daughter gets emotional, do you mirror her or stay calm? What "tricks" allow you to remain a voice of reason? When you stay calm, how does your daughter respond?

3. On a scale of one to ten, how emotionally intelligent is your daughter? How emotionally intelligent are you? What triggers the worst in both of you?

4. Some girls never rein in their emotions. Why does this create trouble?

5. What healthy outlets allow your daughter to work through her emotions and channel them positively?

6. How have your emotions evolved over the years? Are you in a better place than you were five or ten years ago? Do you feel hormonal changes in your body presenting new challenges? Explain.

8

ENJOY HER, LAUGH OFTEN, AND HAVE FUN

I believe that two of the best builders
for self-esteem in kids are for them
to feel safe and to feel enjoyed.
—SISSY GOFF[1]

My Facebook post was titled "20 Things to Do with Your Teenage Daughter."

My friend saw it and acted on my suggestion to invite her daughter on a walk. She knew her daughter felt down, and she hoped the fresh air might lift her spirits.

Her daughter said no because she wasn't in the mood. Though my friend was disappointed, she tried not to take it personally.

Three days later the unexpected happened. Her daughter came to her and asked, "Hey, Mom, you want to go on a walk?" My friend, a single mom of two, was exhausted after a long day at work, but she understood the value of this invitation and made herself go.

It ended up being the best walk. They walked and talked for an hour, surprised they could last that long since neither of them likes to exercise. With excitement in her voice, my friend told me how her daughter shared stories from her life that she'd never mentioned before. It was a meaningful conversation that felt natural, not forced, and they both agreed to go walking again.

I love this story for these takeaways:

1. It is up to us as moms to initiate invitations.
2. We may get shot down, but we can't be disheartened because at the right time, our daughters may respond.
3. When our daughters do respond, we need to be ready and willing to act.

The point of taking a walk—or engaging with your daughter—isn't to get the scoop on her life but to show her you care. If she talks, that's great, but even if she's quiet, you're still building the relationship. You're letting her know you love her and want to spend time together. Your daughter may simply want quiet time in which her brain can shut down and relax. Even if you feel like progress isn't made, it may be exactly what she needs.

Life is too short and too stressful not to enjoy the people you love. Sometimes the best way to bond is to pick up and go, to leave your worries behind and find a change of scenery that allows you to enjoy your daughter like you might a sister or a friend.

Love each other with genuine affection, and take delight in honoring each other.

—ROMANS 12:10 NLT

LET GO OF EXPECTATIONS

I love watching old videos of my kids as babies and toddlers. One video in particular captures the chaos of that season. It is entertaining now, but at the time I felt frustrated.

I'd bought a blow-up pool from Target that I planned for the girls to enjoy one Saturday. They did enjoy it—only not as I'd imagined. When they woke up and spotted the pool in the backyard, they ran outside and headed straight for the water—still in their pajamas. As their clothes got wet, they peeled them off and splashed around naked. The baby was in her diaper, and you know how diapers blow up as they quickly absorb water.

The kids had a blast, but all I could think about was putting them in bathing suits so they could enjoy the pool properly. This scene had upended my plan, yet my husband convinced me to let them play. He saw this moment for what it was and could laugh at the disorder.

Watching that video now as a more seasoned mom, I hear the joy in their squeals and giggles. I see the glee on my daughters' faces as they kick water and dance around. My thoughts are, *Wow, we had fun! Why couldn't I see that at the time? Why did I miss the joy of that day because I wanted a picture-perfect scene?*

Rarely does family life look perfect. Rarely do we get what we imagine as we inflate vinyl pools, plan vacations, or extend invitations. But if we keep our hearts and minds open, we can find joy and humor in the chaos. We can leave room for surprises and not fixate on the glitches that interrupt our plans.

One day I'll look back on *today*. I'll watch videos of my daughters in the teen and tween years. My hope is that I won't feel like I missed the joy of this season. Even when my plans fail, these days are worth treasuring.

This is the day that the L ORD has made; let us rejoice and be glad in it.

—PSALM 118:24 ESV

JOY AND GRIEF

I cried a lot while writing this chapter—more than I've cried in the last five years.

My mom has been sick, and my dad has had health issues too. For nearly four years my mom has been bedridden, and though I'm used to what that means, I still want her to miraculously bounce back. It pains me to see her down.

Watching my kids grow up has wrung my heart as well. As my oldest daughter turned sixteen, she ushered in a new season that left me wrestling with the reality that I will, one by one, need to let my babies go.

I know you have pain in your life, pain that you tuck away and try to save for later. One irony of raising teenagers is that in the very stage when strength is most needed, parents face problems and stress that leave us depleted.

Besides worrying about your teenage daughter, you may worry about these things:

- sick parents
- job security
- health issues
- financial obligations, debt, and paying for college
- marital conflict, divorce, and custody issues
- an ex-husband who harasses you

- the death of loved ones
- the struggles of loved ones
- pressures at work
- changes in relationships
- societal problems
- the future

What nobody told us when our kids were young was how there comes a day when *we are the adults*. *We* are the grown-ups making hard calls. *We* are the ones who get stretched too thin as everyone depends on us.

I believe the torch gets passed in our forties, and while we can certainly find joy in this decade, demands can also wear us down and make us wonder if our joy is over.

Let me be clear: your joy is *not* over. Your best days are still ahead. Through Jesus you have the hope of eternity. You have a problem-free life awaiting you in heaven and the assurance that any earthly trial you face is temporary and not forever.

Thankfully, you also have God's grace. You have a Creator who knows you and understands your needs. What God's grace has shown me is that joy and grief can coexist. I can feel happy and sad on the same day. I can cry after visiting my mom—and laugh with my daughter an hour later. These pockets of joy are gifts that help me see the good in rough seasons.

In the movie *Steel Magnolias*, Dolly Parton's character says, "Laughter through tears is my favorite emotion."[2] When life gets too serious, look for love and humor. Acknowledge your pain but fight for your joy, choosing joy as a spiritual armor that keeps grief from weighing you down.

He will wipe every tear from their eyes, and there will be no more death or sorrow or crying or pain. All these things are gone forever.

—REVELATION 21:4 NLT

ENJOY YOUR DAUGHTER

It doesn't take much to excite a teenager.

My daughter, for instance, hopped in my car one day after cheer practice with her friend Ellie. They were starving and exhausted, and when they mentioned a craving for queso and quesadillas, I called in an order to their favorite Mexican restaurant. Minutes later we picked up the food, and as they scarfed it down, you would have thought I'd taken them to Paris. They were over-the-moon ecstatic, so happy about this surprise that ignited a second wind.

It was money well spent.

Enjoying your daughter shouldn't be complicated. Her life is complicated already, so keep it simple. Focus on what she likes—an Icee, a Greek salad, her favorite body spray or flowers in her bedroom—and pick a day to surprise her. Pay attention to the little joys that make her happy.

I have another daughter who loves chocolate chip cookies. While shopping one day, I bumped into a friend who had a box of freshly baked chocolate chip cookies from a nearby store. It reminded me of my daughter and an argument we had that morning.

I bought a cookie as a peace offering to remind my daughter that even when we knock heads, I still love her. I set the bag on our kitchen countertop, and when she arrived home an hour later, she came straight into my office and asked about it.

"Mom, who's that cookie for?"

"It's for you," I said. "I'm sorry I was so hard on you earlier."

For a moment my daughter stayed silent. Then a slow, knowing smile crept up her face, and I knew she was touched. That cookie opened the door for us to hug, talk, and make up. It taught me the value of a creative apology that speaks to my child's heart.

Will I always buy cookies as peace offerings? No. But I will pay attention to what my girls love and look for chances to show them I've noticed.

Deep inside every girl's heart is a desire to feel seen, known, and loved. As smart and beautiful as your daughter is, she's surrounded by smart and beautiful girls. She often feels like another face in the crowd—overlooked, unappreciated, and maybe even invisible.

By enjoying her, you single her out. You remind her that her life matters; she is worth spending time with and getting to know. This gives her a glimpse of how God enjoys her (and *you*) and smiles at His creation.

You and your daughter both need joy, peace, and laughter in your lives. Following are ways to find these things together.

Thirty-Five Ways to Enjoy Your Teenage Daughter

1. Take a special trip, just the two of you, to enjoy a new adventure.
2. Try a Zumba, yoga, or SoulCycle class together, going in with a sense of humor and ready to laugh at yourself.
3. Watch a late-night movie with her, waiting until ten o'clock or whenever the rest of the household has gone to sleep so it feels like you're in a private world.
4. Do a charcoal mask with her, or get makeovers at the cosmetics store.

5. Stop by her room before bed and pray over her. Pray for God's protection and favor in her life. Thank God for choosing you as her mother. Ask your daughter how you can help her this week.

6. Give her a cookbook and ask her to pick out a healthy new recipe you can make, and taste-test it together.

7. Find a place to go bowling or to ride go-karts.

8. When it's tryout time, make it her special week. Fix whatever she wants for breakfast, pick her up from clinic with a smoothie, and cover her mirror with Post-it notes that have encouraging words, quotes, or Bible verses.

9. Take her to a cool sushi restaurant.

10. Get manicures or pedicures together before a vacation or special event.

11. Go on a walk after dinner.

12. Take her shopping with the primary intent of learning what her style is—and what she feels good wearing—so you can shop for her in the future.

13. Take her with you to visit a friend who has a new baby, and bond over the sweetness of that baby wrapped in a pink or blue bundle.

14. Take her to a coffee shop. This can be a fun outing or a change of scenery, a place where she does homework while you read a book.

15. Challenge her to a game of tennis.

16. Play a board game or cards.

17. Pull out a special dress from your past (like your wedding dress or rehearsal dinner dress) and have her try it on for fun.

18. Text her funny videos and memes. One that I recently shared with my girls: "Having a daughter is like having a little broke best friend who thinks you're rich."

19. Show her pictures and videos from her childhood, and tell

the stories behind the memories. Describe the moments when you first realized her strengths and disposition.

20. Reward her after a stressful week or a big test by having her favorite treat waiting at home.

21. Surprise her. It could be a surprise party, a surprise gift on her pillow (such as cute earrings), or a surprise *yes!* when she expects to hear *no*. One teenager told me about her mom surprising her for a trip she took with friends by packing snacks for everyone and a cute new blouse inside her suitcase.

22. Plan a reverse surprise birthday party, where you surprise her guests by unexpectedly picking them up at their homes (their moms know the plan ahead of time) and taking them to breakfast or dinner.

23. Take her to see her favorite artist in concert, getting tickets with her friends and their moms.

24. Paint pottery together.

25. Take a cake decorating class.

26. Start family traditions like wearing matching pajamas on Christmas Eve, getting breakfast in bed on your birthdays, visiting a sunflower field every summer, carving pumpkins the night before Halloween, going around the dinner table to name the "rose" and the "thorn" of your day, taking pictures at the pumpkin patch, or building a fire on the first day of winter.

27. Once a seasonal item is available—like Christmas peppermint ice cream—make a run to the store to get it.

28. Be playful, lighten up, and laugh at yourself. Blare eighties music and show her your Michael Jackson moonwalk or your dance to Duran Duran. Watch funny videos on YouTube.

29. Smile at her, wink at her, offer a high five as she walks by. When she shares good news—like a high test score that she's proud of—give her a fist bump and tell her how happy it makes you to see her hard work pay off.

30. Have snacks waiting on the countertop after school or when she and her friends come to your house. (Food will instantly win over teenagers, and queso is always a hit!)
31. Volunteer together, leading a small group at church or serving at a nonprofit that helps women and children.
32. Leave room for spontaneity. My daughter and I spent a weekend in Asheville, North Carolina, before she went to summer camp, and one of her favorite moments was sitting together under a tree and talking. This unscripted bonding meant more to her than a fancy dinner that night.
33. Spend a Saturday at the farmers market, buying fresh produce and talking to artisans and farmers.
34. Take hikes and pack a lunch to enjoy while overlooking a scenic view.
35. Turn college visits into fun road trips, playing her favorite song list in the car, trying popular restaurants, and timing your visit around a special game, festival, or event.

In *The Back Door to Your Teen's Heart*, the authors write,

> One of the main reasons it is difficult to enjoy adolescents is that they don't seem to enjoy us. They no longer have the need they once had for our time and attention. They're embarrassed to spend time with us in public. . . . But biblical love *is* about caring for those who are difficult to love. It is active, not passive. It pursues. For those of us in relationships with adolescents, this is our challenge. Whether they are enjoying us or not, we still need to enjoy them.[3]

Parents need thick skin when parenting teenagers. You never know if your daughter will jump on an invitation or reject it. Either way, keep trying. Keep inviting her to walk, inviting her to dinner, asking her to try something fun. Let her know you enjoy her company so she feels like an enjoyable person.

Emotion follows motion, and when you act like you love your daughter even if you don't wholeheartedly feel it at the moment, the real emotion will follow.

I know grown women who are still waiting for their mothers to enjoy them, so send that message now. Enjoy your daughter and open the door to laughter, harmony, and heartfelt connection.

———————— • ————————

Sarah said, "God has brought me laughter, and everyone who hears about this will laugh with me."
–GENESIS 21:6

———————— • ————————

BE PRESENT

My father often says the perk of being a grandparent is having less pressure. After all, grandparents can enjoy their grandkids without having to teach them, correct them, or earn a living. It can be all fun and games. Your parenting years, on the other hand, are also your working years. You juggle many demands as you raise kids, which makes it harder to focus.

And while small kids are physically exhausting, big kids are mentally exhausting. Some days my brain short-circuits as my four daughters head in four different directions and I constantly think ahead so I don't miss a beat.

Here is the problem with that: God is found in the present. Not the future, not the past, but the *present*. One reason I often miss God—and the joy in store today—is because I'm busy and distracted by what must be done tomorrow.

In *The Screwtape Letters*, C. S. Lewis says that God wants

us to attend chiefly to two things: eternity and the present. He writes, "In a word, the Future is, of all things, the thing *least like* eternity."[4]

Lewis explains that God wants us to obey the present voice, bear the present cross, receive the present grace, and give thanks for the present pleasure. There is a holiness in today that can't be found by looking back or looking ahead, and the way to encounter God is to live in the present and think about eternity.

What does this mean for you and your daughter? Two things:

1. Regretting the past—or romanticizing the past, always wishing to go back—can keep you from fully enjoying her.
2. Fixating on the future—with your worries *or* your fantasies—can also keep you from fully enjoying her.

The sweet spot is in the middle. To think about the future as it relates to eternity, but to focus your attention on today and the girl who's right in front of you and growing up before your eyes.

God wants you to enjoy your daughter. He wants your relationship to feel like a blessing, not a burden. Joy begins with gratitude, so thank God for the gift of her. Thank Him for His love. Trust Him with this relationship, and know that He is working behind the scenes, letting no invitation or act of love go to waste because all play into a greater purpose.

Take delight in the LORD, and he will give you the desires of your heart.

—PSALM 37:4

REFLECTION QUESTIONS

. . . .

1. When your daughter rejects an invitation to be with you, do you take it personally or move on and try again later?

2. What life stressors weigh heavily on your heart? How can you lighten your load and fight for joy?

3. What activities or interests draw you and your daughter closer? What new activity can you attempt?

4. What makes your daughter great company? What traits emerge in her (and you) when it's just you two?

5. What are your family traditions? Are there traditions you started when your daughter was a baby or little girl? Are there traditions you'd like to start now? Explain.

6. Describe a spontaneous moment with your daughter that felt magical. Why does living in the present lead to unexpectedly special moments?

. . . .

TAKE CARE OF YOURSELF AND HAVE A SUPPORT SYSTEM FOR HARD DAYS

Adolescence is about more than
our teen's ability to change; it is also
about our own ability to grow.
—DR. MADELINE LEVINE[1]

I was on my back porch having quiet time with God when the tears started. I let them flow because it felt cathartic to be vulnerable. God knows me inside out, and as I admitted my worries and the sense of failure in my heart, I sensed Him saying, *Quit talking about how you're falling short, and just let Me love you.*

And that's when I broke down.

It was early morning, and the whole house was asleep. Minutes later, my daughter stumbled downstairs. She was sleepy and slow-moving, and as she noticed me on the porch through the glass door, she stared for a long moment. Then she walked toward me.

Oh no, I thought, *she sees me upset, and now she'll ask what's wrong. I guess I'll be honest.*

My girls have seen me cry before, but not often, so I expected my daughter to open the porch door and show concern. Instead, she opened the door, stared at me blankly, and asked a question I didn't expect:

"Mom, will you make me breakfast?"

Really? I wanted to reply. *That's your response? Your mother is visibly upset, and you want breakfast?*

I took a deep breath and told her I'd fix breakfast after I finished my quiet time. She nodded and slipped back inside. Her lack of compassion seemed out of character, so I tried not to read into it. Maybe her brain was still asleep. Maybe hunger made her oblivious. Or maybe she was just acting her age.

Whatever the case, this incident reminded me how we moms need love and support beyond our nuclear family. We need support systems and passions that nurture us as women, not just as parents.

It is no secret that our children don't always make us feel good. They aren't always attuned or sensitive to our feelings. And during the teenage years (also called the "narcissistic years" by therapists), they can be exceptionally self-centered.

Chances are, your daughter isn't thinking about your needs, and that makes it imperative for you to think about them yourself. Do what it takes to stay healthy and strong—to keep yourself in a good place for the sake of your sanity, your health, and your family.

———— • ————

"I will refresh the weary and satisfy the faint."
—JEREMIAH 31:25

———— • ————

LEARN TO MOTHER YOURSELF

My sorority sister was in town for a funeral.

A high school friend had lost her dad, and this was her *ninth* funeral to attend in six months. All her friends were losing parents, and we talked about how this is, sadly, our current stage in life.

I have another friend whose mom has dementia. While she's thankful her mom is alive, she misses the strong Southern woman who raised her.

"I just wish she'd call me," she says, "and tell me to get off the couch and quit being lazy. She was funny like that, and I miss it."

When my husband and I married in our twenties, we entered the wedding season of life. We had a party every weekend as our friends got hitched.

In our thirties, those friends got pregnant, and the celebrations continued as we entered the baby season of life.

Now in our forties, the theme is funerals. Our friends are either losing parents (my husband has lost his dad) or taking care of sick parents.

This isn't a joyful, party-filled season. There is no playbook to go by as the roles reverse and the generation ahead of us starts to depend on us, slip away, or take on new roles as caregivers.

It's ironic that when we need our parents most—while raising teenagers and watching them leave the nest—they face their own challenges and stressors that take them away from us. They can't drop everything and support us like they did when our kids were babies because they're dealing with health scares, memory loss, doctor appointments, chronic pain, or other issues.

It can feel strange when your mother no longer nags you to see a doctor for your cough, your father no longer obsesses over the safety of your car, and you're not sure who to call when your teenager tests you and you need someone older and wiser—who adores you and your child—to give advice.

If your parents are healthy, praise God. Thank Him for that gift, and make memories with your parents while you can. One day these memories will feel like a treasure.

If your parents are sick or deceased, know that you are not alone. Many people ride in that boat, parenting kids while caring for parents and missing their parental rock.

Last year, a mom who planned an event for me said she wanted to "mother me" during my visit with a restful retreat in her guesthouse. I almost dropped the phone and hopped on a plane to meet her because the thought of being "mothered" sounded heavenly. Like many moms, I'm often thinking about the needs of others, and it felt wonderful to have the tables turned.

The older I get—and the more responsibilities I shoulder— the more self-care I need. This is true for you as well. Life requires more of you today than it did five years ago, and if all you ever do is give, you'll get depleted. Your wheels will fall off. You'll feel tired, numb, and vulnerable.

For this reason, I believe in learning to mother yourself. Making sure that *you* don't fall through the cracks or get in the habit of self-neglect.

How? By tending to and protecting your health. Doing things that build strength and stamina. Cultivating a life that you enjoy. Making sure you feel equipped to handle the challenges of adolescence.

Here are some tips for self-care in your current season of life.

Twelve Ways to "Mother" Yourself

1. Keep your wellness appointments.

It's easy and tempting to cancel these, especially when you feel and appear healthy, but prevention and early detection can add years to your life.

2. See a doctor when needed.

I once had a cold that lasted a month. I tried to push through it, but it only got worse. When my husband finally made me go to the doctor, I learned that I had walking pneumonia. I was so mad at myself for letting a small problem escalate into a big one.

3. Exercise.

I discovered exercise in college as a stress reliever, and I still need it for mental health. It benefits my brain even more than my body. I believe that of all the activities I've tried, anyone can benefit from walking and Pilates. Try them with a friend for thirty minutes, and then gradually add more time.

4. Stop beating yourself up.

The script you play in your head matters. What you tell yourself matters. When you mentally abuse yourself, you parent with insecurity, fear, and despair. Every mistake feels like a final defeat. But as Lysa TerKeurst says, "Bad moments don't make bad moms."[2] God's grace is bigger than any defeat, and through Him you can parent with confidence and hope, rewriting the script in your head.

5. Treat bad days as good data.

When you have bad days, bad feelings, or bad experiences, ask yourself, *What can I learn from this? What might God be trying to teach me?* My bad days teach me about humility, compassion, and deeper dependence on Him.

6. Don't dwell on regrets.

Yesterday is gone. You can't change it, but you can change today. You can pioneer a new path. In a study I did on Saint Paul's letters to the Philippians, we talked about Paul's change of heart on the road to Damascus. Once God opened Paul's eyes to the evil he was doing, Paul went from persecuting Christians to spreading the gospel worldwide. He was unstoppable, carrying out his new mission as a completely forgiven man. God wants you to live that way too—as a completely forgiven woman on a mission for Him.

7. Create your team.

You can find advice about raising small children anywhere. Any mom can share stories about potty training or helping their little ones sleep through the night. As your kids grow up, however, you can't share their issues publicly. You learn to confide in fewer people and choose advisers you can trust. It's okay to have a small circle of consultants. Choose friends whom you admire and respect, and include some trained professionals—a pastor, spiritual adviser, or therapist—who give good insight and advice.

8. Seek healthy outlets for your pain.

After losing a child to suicide, one family removed all alcohol from their home so they would rely on two things only: God and each other. They understood human weakness and the desperation for quick fixes when pain runs deep.

When you face pain in your life, lean on your faith and your relationships. Let love carry you, and you'll emerge stronger on the other side.

9. Share your struggles with loved ones.

Problems are isolating. They make you feel alone, ashamed, and tempted to withdraw. The enemy wants this. He wants you to suffer alone so you'll start to believe his lies. Don't fall for his tricks; instead of turning inward, turn outward. Bring your struggles to light. Admit them to people who can speak truth and pray for you.

As the authors of *Boundaries* explain, "Evil can take over the empty house of our souls. Even when our lives seem to be in order, isolation guarantees spiritual vulnerability. It's only when our house is full of the love of God and others that we can resist the wiles of the Devil. Plugging in is neither an option, nor a luxury; it is a spiritual and emotional life-and-death issue."[3] No matter how strong you feel, you need people to help you through your darkest and hardest hours.

10. Get enough sleep, and don't overcommit.

I'll never be a writer who publishes a book every year. To do so, I'd have to live on four hours of sleep a night and double my workload. I know myself. I'd be perpetually grumpy and stressed. It's not worth it because it would ruin my relationships. Know yourself too. Set limits for what you can and can't do. This act of self-love helps ensure that you don't sacrifice the wrong things.

11. Be a blessing.

Many people spend the first half of life looking inward, getting to know themselves, and the second half of their life looking outward, searching for ways to help others. Spiritual maturity begins when you realize that you are here to serve. Rather than asking God to bless you, ask to be the blessing, the answer to someone's prayer. Find ways to "mother" others as you mother yourself. Ironically, it's through serving and using your gifts that you discover real purpose and joy.

12. Accept and reflect God's love.

In *The Return of the Prodigal Son*, author Henri Nouwen says that becoming the compassionate father is the ultimate goal of the spiritual life. As we mature, we move past being the prodigal son and the jealous brother to become the merciful father who stretches out his hand in blessing and receives his children with compassion regardless of how they feel or think about him.[4]

This book helped me understand how our generation is transitioning into the father role. While this role doesn't feel natural quite yet, God will continue shaping our hearts and preparing us for the day when we can model His selfless love.

Raising teenagers while mourning parents isn't for the faint of heart. While death is the theme of this stage, our God is a God of life. He gives us hope and a future. He refreshes the weary.

God keeps His word and lives up to His promises. When life beats you down—when you feel discouraged, defeated, or ill-equipped—pray for renewal, asking Him to comfort you, strengthen you, and most importantly, stay close to you.

———— • ————

Weeping may last through the night, but joy comes with the morning.

—PSALMS 30:5 NLT

———— • ————

LIFE BEYOND YOUR DAUGHTER

"My daughter told me I need to get a life," my friend shared with me as we took a road trip together, and we laughed because her daughter is in sixth grade.

Like many girls her age, she is pulling away and craving more time with friends. She adores her mom, yet she's excited about her independence.

Chances are, you had a life before you had kids. You had interests, passions, and the energy to stay awake past ten o'clock at night. But having a baby shifted your priorities. You became perfectly content nesting at home and marveling over your miracle.

As your baby grew up—especially if siblings came along—life became a circus. Some days your only goal was survival. You *had* to put things on the back burner. In the tween and teen years, the busyness doubled as different people had to be in different places at the same time: a dance competition, a birthday party, a friend's house, and a mandatory practice.

Gone were the days of keeping one schedule as a family, taking the whole crew to the park and calling it a day.

I don't regret any time I've spent with my kids or invested in their lives. When I look back, I'm glad that my husband and I have made our family a priority.

What I recognize, however, is how today's culture of all-in parenting often veers toward unhealthy extremes. While it's great that we engage in our kids' lives—too much parental involvement is better than too little—going overboard can create an imbalance in our adult lives.

Somehow we've become a generation of parents who wrap our lives around our kids—often to the detriment of ourselves, our marriage, and the family unit.

Dr. Madeline Levine discusses this dynamic in *Teach Your Children Well*: "We hunker down and immerse ourselves in our children's activities at the expense of our adult relationships and our own continued development. Decreasing the sphere of our own lives makes us increasingly dependent on our children for a sense of meaning and accomplishment."[5]

This passage speaks to me. I think one reason we see anxiety among children and despair among parents is because our kids feel the weight of our expectations as we often rely on them to make us happy. They carry burdens they aren't meant to carry when we make them our ultimate source of joy.

God wants Jesus to be our ultimate source of joy. He created us to be Christ-centered parents, not child-centered parents. With Jesus at the center of our universe, we can have hope apart from our children. We can widen the sphere of our adult lives, defining ourselves—first and foremost—as children of God.

Being a mom is important, but you are far more than a mom. As Sissy Goff says, it's good for your kids to see you as a multifaceted woman: "Yes, your heart is interconnected with the heart of your child. But you are still you. And they need you to be. They need you to have hope outside of them. And ultimately, any real hope comes from the fact that God has poured out His love into our hearts—and theirs."[6]

When my oldest girls became teenagers and started to pull away, I realized that I'd wrapped my life around them. My instinct was to become clingy, to pull back my center of gravity, but that drove them away. They needed space, and as I gave them space, they came back to me on their own terms. I didn't have to force the connection.

Parenting teenagers is like being on call. They don't need you all the time, but when they do need you, they want you close by and available. My goal is to be available for my girls while also stepping back, unwrapping myself from their world and broadening my own world. Tending to things I put on the back burner, like old friendships and interests.

Your teenage daughter needs space, and so do you. Healthy relationships have breathing room, and it's easier to give her breathing room when you have additional sources of joy.

How do you find these additional sources? How do you broaden your world beyond your role as a mom? By tending to three things:

1. Your interests and passions
2. Your adult relationships
3. Your identity

INTERESTS AND PASSIONS

I started writing as an escape from my young children.

It was my healthy escape because Plan B was a bottle of wine every night. With three kids under the age of four and a husband who worked until eight o'clock every weeknight, I had days when I felt like I was losing my mind. I needed a hobby to help me decompress and feel like my old self again.

I would write once my husband got home from work and took over family duties. I aimed for fifteen minutes, but many nights I stayed up past midnight, unable to stop typing. I knew I'd found my passion when my family went out of town without me one weekend and I wrote for twelve hours straight.

God has planted passions in your heart too, passions to use for good. Whatever brings you to life, makes you lose track of time, or simply piques your curiosity deserves close attention. Passion leads to purpose, and through your passions God reveals Himself and uses you to impact others.

Your passion may be obvious. You may know that cooking, art, medicine, health, fashion, design, caregiving, teaching, flying, or managing money is your thing. You may have a happy place that restores your soul: the beach, the great outdoors, a tennis court, a stage, or a bike in a spin class. You may have healthy escapes that fill your tank and boost your spirits when life gets you down.

If you haven't found a passion yet, keep exploring. Try new hobbies and adventures for fun, and don't worry about being good. If you enjoy an activity, you'll learn the ropes. Raw talent is great, but a strong work ethic and a willingness to learn more can also take you far.

Often when I feel discouraged as a mom, God blesses me through my interests and passions. On the same day that my daughter acts cold or distant, I may receive an email from a mom thanking me for my book or a blog post. God's timing is perfect, and it's nice to feel appreciated beyond your family and home.

"You are the light of the world. A town built on a hill cannot be hidden. Neither do people light a lamp and put it under a bowl. Instead they put it on its stand, and it gives light to everyone in the house. In the same way, let your light shine before others, that they may see your good deeds and glorify your Father in heaven."

–MATTHEW 5:14–16

ADULT RELATIONSHIPS

Adults need adults for the same reason that teens need teens. Nobody "gets" you like one of your own.

At every age, peer relationships matter. And when raising a teenager, you need adult relationships that bring you comfort, joy, and strength. You need trustworthy people in your corner—your friends, your sister, your husband, your parents, your favorite coworker, your therapist, maybe even your hairdresser—who serve as a sounding board, a rock, and emotional support.

Because if you're parenting correctly, you'll make your teenager mad some days.

You'll get pushback on certain decisions.

You'll deal with complaints and bad attitudes.

You'll feel lonely, lost, unloved, defeated, or unsettled.

You'll wish you didn't care, because not caring or making them carry out their commitments or even having rules would make your life so much easier (at least for now).

In the Bible, Moses received help from his peers during battle (Exodus 17:11–13). When Moses held up his hands, Israel prevailed, but when Moses let down his hands, Amalek prevailed. As Moses' hands grew tired, Aaron and Hur sat him on a stone. They supported Moses' hands and kept them steady on each side until the sun had set—and Israel won.

Moses was a powerful leader, yet even he needed trusted friends and advisers. He won the battle by humbling himself and admitting that his strength was not enough.

Sometimes your strength isn't enough either. Sometimes you face a battle, in your heart or your home, that calls for extra resources. Sometimes you need a distraction, adult interaction that makes you laugh and feel free.

A strong friendship can bolster you, and so can a strong marriage. Investing in them is an investment in your future because your friends and your spouse (if you're married) will still be present as your kids leave home. They know you and your history, and they can offer honest feedback. Especially when you're at odds with your daughter, they can tell you if you're being too hard, too soft, too prideful, too acquiescent—or if you're right on target. They can tell you if you're right to stand your ground and help you wait out the storm.

On a good day, a support system is a bonus. On a bad day, it's a lifeline.

Your support system will look different from mine, but we both need them. And since you never know what another mom is facing, what battles she's fighting, or how she's being treated at home, show compassion, grace, and love. Listen without judgment, give her space to be real, and circle the wagons in times of distress, lending your strength as she needs it.

Two are better than one, because they have a good return for their labor: If either of them falls down, one can help the other up. But pity anyone who falls and has no one to help them up.

–ECCLESIASTES 4:9–10

IDENTITY

The first time my daughter tried out for cheerleading, I felt like *I* was trying out for cheerleading.

After all, I'd shared the journey with her. I'd driven her to every lesson, seen every emotion, and witnessed her hard work. I knew about her mental blocks, self-doubt, and love for the sport. I knew that if she didn't make the squad, she'd be heartbroken. We'd get through it, of course, but only after a downpour of tears and days of self-doubt.

My husband loves our daughter as much as I do, yet he stayed detached. He wasn't emotionally invested in her dreams because he hadn't seen the details in the making. For him, trying to understand cheer tryouts would be like me trying to understand an intense football game that he's watched for three hours when I enter the room with only a minute left on the scoreboard.

We root for the same team, yet his emotions and adrenaline are high. He's on the brink of a heart attack after watching the epic plays and horrific blunders of our team. He's emotionally invested in a way that I'm not because I entered late in the game. I don't know the backstory that led to the heart-pounding final moments.

Every family is different, but in many cases, moms know the details. We see, hear, and witness many events that integrate us deeply into our children's world. While this engagement is good, we can get overly invested and blur the line between the end of our children and the beginning of ourselves.

Rather than find your identity in Christ, you may find your identity in your child and jump on the emotional roller coaster that ties your joy and self-worth to:

- the choices your daughter makes,
- the emotions she feels,
- how she makes you look as a parent, and
- how she makes you feel.

Clearly, this is dangerous territory. And what becomes evident during adolescence, as your daughter starts to cut ties and expand her world, is how she is her own person finding her own way.

She'll make some choices you don't agree with.

She'll hurt you, disappoint you, and let you down at times.

She'll experience rejections and disappointments that she wants you to care about, but not to the point where you're so upset that you can't offer hope and strength.

Rooting your identity in Jesus allows you to journey beside

your daughter with a healthy sense of self. It unites your joy to what He did on the cross, not what your daughter is doing, feeling, or saying today. She is her own person, and so are you. Count on God to give you strength, and then share that strength with your daughter.

If anyone is in Christ, the new creation has come: The old has gone, the new is here!

–2 CORINTHIANS 5:17

LET GOD LOVE YOU

Some days I can't do anything right, not even a ponytail.

On the morning of my daughter's first homecoming pep rally, she needed my help with french-braiding her hair into a high ponytail. I felt confident in this small task, yet after four attempts, it still looked lumpy. As her ride to school honked outside, my daughter's eyes filled with tears, my eyes filled with tears, and she hurried out the door saying that she'd get a friend to do it.

She and her team had worked tirelessly for weeks to prepare for this day. They were exhausted, nervous, and emotionally fragile. I wanted to calm her stress, yet I'd only amplified it. Rather than dwell in mom guilt, I reminded myself of this: *God loves me, even when I'm off my game. I can always rest in His love.*

God loves you too. His love is a rock, a security blanket you can carry through every up and down.

How do you let God love you? How do you feel His love when your mind is consumed with worries, fears, or *far* bigger errors than getting your daughter's hair right? By remembering these ten truths.

1. **God's love looks different from human love.** It doesn't fluctuate with your performance, your circumstances, or His mood. God is for you, and nothing can separate you from His love that is in Jesus (Romans 8:31–39).

2. **God is always available and ready to grow a relationship with you.** If you come close to Him, He'll come close to you (Romans 8:18).

3. **God's power is made perfect in weakness.** Your weaknesses are His opportunity to do His best work. You can boast of your weaknesses so that Christ's power rests on you (2 Corinthians 12:9).

4. **When God forgives, He forgets.** After you confess your sins, He wants you to move on and live as a fully forgiven woman (Hebrews 8:12).

5. **God knows every detail about you—and loves you still.** He knows your heart, your pain, your thoughts, and your words before you speak. His love is greater than human knowledge, too big to comprehend (Psalm 139:1–4; Deuteronomy 31:8; Ephesians 3:18–19).

6. **God is the ultimate comforter, rescuer, and deliverer.** He comforts you in affliction so you can comfort others. He goes before you and with you, never leaving you or abandoning you. He can deliver you from the pit of despair and put your feet on solid ground (2 Corinthians 1:3–5; Deuteronomy 31:8; Psalm 40:2).

7. **God understands your humanity.** He is aware of how you want to do good but often don't, and how you don't want to do what's wrong but often do it anyway. He designed you to need Him and gives you the desire and the power to do what pleases Him (Romans 7:19; Philippians 2:13).

8. **Suffering isn't forever.** After you have suffered a little while,

God will restore you, making you strong, firm, and steadfast (1 Peter 5:10).

9. **God rewards faithfulness in His time.** The good you do today will reap a harvest if you don't give up (Galatians 6:9).

10. **God created you to live in community.** He loves you and strengthens you through other people (Proverbs 27:17; Ecclesiastes 4:9).

Perfect parents don't prepare their kids for an imperfect world. While it's important to set a positive example, your daughter learns just as much (if not more) from the way you deal with the unexpected. How you handle your inadequacies, fears, trials, and problems teaches her about resiliency, coping skills, and digging deep to find strength. It instills a reference point she can turn to when she faces trials and stress in her life.

Right now your plate is full. There is only so much you can take off to reduce your load. You need strength, so protect your physical, mental, and spiritual strength. Conserve energy for what matters most. Invest in hobbies and passions that feed your soul.

You also need encouraging friends, so be an encouraging friend to others. Extend help on your good days, and receive help on your bad days. Nobody understands your current situation quite like other moms, so find solidarity in that village. Most importantly, keep your eyes on God. Let Him love you, renew you, and guide you. As the author of your story, He can be trusted with this chapter—and every one that follows.

---·---

"Nothing will be impossible with God."
–LUKE 1:37 ESV

---·---

REFLECTION QUESTIONS

1. Name a time when you felt lonely, ignored, or misunderstood as a mom of a teenager. What, if anything, brought you comfort?

2. What makes you happy beyond your children? What adult relationships would you like to deepen to prepare for the empty-nester years?

3. Why is self-care essential for moms? How can we "mother" each other during this season of losing our parents?

4. "On a good day, a support system is a bonus. On a bad day, it's a lifeline." Do you agree? How can women build encouraging, uplifting communities?

5. Is there a secret dream in your heart? What passion would you pursue if you weren't afraid to fail?

6. Do you believe God loves you and wants you to rest in His love? Why or why not?

. . . .

· 10 · · · · · · · · · · · · · · · · ·

PRAY FOR HER AND EMPOWER HER THROUGH FAITH

Your daughter needs God for
two reasons: she needs help
and she needs hope.
—DR. MEG MEEKER[1]

When my daughter was two years old, she went into anaphylactic shock. It was a terrifying and painful reminder of how life can change in a blink.

We'd been vigilant about her food allergies, yet this was a new allergy that she'd never been tested for. My hands shook as I dialed 911 and they told me to administer the EpiPen.

I'll never forget the pulsating fear that spanned my body as I ran my baby down a dark and steep driveway to the paramedic van at the street. Having no sight of her face in the pitch-black night amplified my fear, and I could only pray the EpiPen had worked to stop her swelling face and tightening throat.

By God's grace, that EpiPen did work, but that night changed me. It was my third major parenting scare, one that left me shaken for days and ready to bargain with God.

I didn't like how different my faith looked *before* a scare versus *after* a scare. It felt wrong. Why did it take an emergency to bring me to my knees? Why did I regret the way I forgot God on normal days and clung to Him in a crisis?

Deep down, I knew I depended on Him for every breath in my lungs, yet I felt self-sufficient until a crisis hit. Seeing my child in danger—and feeling helpless to save her—made it extremely clear that I have far less control than I believe.

C. S. Lewis said, "I pray because I can't help myself. I pray because I'm helpless. I pray because the need flows out of me all the time—waking and sleeping. It doesn't change God—it changes me."[2] The purpose of prayer isn't to manipulate God or treat Him like a magic genie, but to deepen our relationship with Him. Through trials and triumphs, we can draw closer and lean on Him for wisdom, comfort, direction, peace, courage, strength, and protection.

The teenage years usher in a panoply of stress. As one worry settles down, a new one pops up. There is so much to worry about—new drivers, underage drinking, binge drinking, drugs, drugs slipped into drinks, sexual activity, sexual assault, suicide, still-developing brains, bad influences, life-changing mistakes, anxiety, loneliness, social media, and a thousand other concerns—and all weigh heavy on a mother's heart.

We want guarantees, but there is no guarantee that a teenager thriving at 8:00 a.m. will still be thriving by 8:00 p.m. that night. For those who crave certainty, this can be paralyzing.

The good news is, we have an almighty God. He holds the

world (and our teenagers) in His hand, and He knows this job is too big for us to handle alone. He created us to need Him and to give Him our burdens. He hears our prayers, and He promises that our prayers don't return void. He works all things together for good for those who love Him (Romans 8:28).

The teen years hold *tremendous potential* to turn mothers into prayer warriors. This season can amplify our prayer lives and embolden our faith unlike any other period. Our daughters will face trials that we can't control, predict, or fix. We won't always be present when they need us, but God will be. He hears our prayers and cares more about our daughters than we do.

Even if you're new to faith, even if you're walking only one step ahead of your daughter, you can be a powerful prayer warrior. You can equip her spiritually and point her to the One who gives everlasting peace.

———————— • ————————

This is the confidence we have in approaching God: that if we ask anything according to his will, he hears us.

–1 JOHN 5:14

———————— • ————————

PARENTING WITHOUT GUARANTEES

I once read a parenting book that frustrated me. The wisdom was amazing, but it felt like the author was saying, "I raised great kids, and here's how you can too." There were many $1 + 1 + 1 = 3$ insinuations like:

Taking Kids to Church + Studying God's Word + Surrounding Them with Godly People = Godly Kids Set for Life

I believe in intentional parenting, and that's why I wrote this book. I believe it's hard to love someone you don't really know, and for our daughters to know and love God, it's important that we take them to church, help them understand Scripture, cultivate character, and encourage healthy relationships.

But what parenting books often ignore (or skim over) is the fact that even the best parenting doesn't guarantee results. Jesus was the perfect teacher, yet one of his disciples betrayed him. His perfection could not override the free will that God gives everyone.

Also, a child who looks like a role model can be more distant from God than a child whose life is in shambles but who has a deep, desperate faith. A girl who thrives in her twenties may self-destruct in her forties. There is no guarantee that any child is set for life, even if they're well-adjusted as they leave home.

Cameron Cole, a youth pastor in the same church for fifteen years, wrote an interesting article for Rooted Ministry titled "Mystery and Lament: When It Looks Like Your Child's Life Is Falling Apart." He talks about God's long-game vision and waiting patiently for Him to act.

Cameron says,

> I have seen the sweet, "good," youth ministry insider—the type who answers every question in Sunday school and never misses a youth event—become the pot-smoking atheist. I have seen the rebellious high schooler become a Jesus-loving man of the Gospel, the quietly skeptical girl become a consistent church-goer in college, and the kid with superstar Christian parents never give Christianity a second thought.[3]

Cameron adds that God makes no guarantees in this life, but regardless of how messy, painful, and hopeless things look, God is at work in your child's life. He pursues your child, and whether she realizes it or participates in it, He'll use her life for His ultimate glory. As we accept the unpredictable nature of God's redemptive work, we will gain patience in challenging moments.

This is real life. This acknowledges how today is one chapter in a much bigger story, and though we can't see ahead, we can stay faithful in praying and never give up on our daughters *or* on God.

My friend's husband often says, "The older our kids get, the more we go to God about our children than we go to our children about God." Some of our best work as parents is done on our knees. Sometimes what our kids need most is less talk and more prayers.

Like C. S. Lewis, I pray because I'm helpless. I need the grace of heaven to deal with the uncertainty of this world. I can't control my daughters or their lives, but I can pray for them and empower them through faith. You can, too, praying for your girl with confidence and courage.

Devote yourselves to prayer with an alert mind and a thankful heart.

—COLOSSIANS 4:2 NLT

BECOME HER PRAYER WARRIOR

Teenage girls are hungry for comfort and reassurance. When I speak to a group, I hear it in their voices and see it in their eyes, a look of searching and a longing to make sense of life.

They want an anchor. They need a rock they can count on. In a season when everything in their life constantly changes—their feelings, moods, bodies, relationships, and circumstances—they crave security.

This is where God comes in. This is where we can tell them that people and life are always subject to change, but God isn't.

He is the same yesterday, today, and tomorrow. He pursues them relentlessly and yearns for a relationship. They can lose everything they love on earth, but they can't lose His love. God is the security they're searching for, the anchor for their soul, the One who saves them through Jesus.

Psalm 127:4 says children are like arrows in the hands of a warrior. As parents, we shape our arrows and send them into the future. We decide where to aim. The goal is to launch Christ followers, to raise girls who know their purpose and will influence their generation and the following generations for Him.

God can use our daughters in ways that outlive our time on earth, and when we stay mindful of this, we find extra motivation to impact tomorrow through our parenting and prayers today.

Here are prayers to say as your daughter's prayer warrior.

Fifty Prayers for Your Teenage Daughter

1. Pray for her to be a light—and for God's armor to protect her.
2. Pray for her heart to be like Jesus' heart.
3. Pray for wise counsel, healthy-minded friends, and godly advisers.
4. Pray for God to protect her physically, mentally, emotionally, and spiritually.
5. Pray for her health.
6. Pray for your daughter to have the courage to do what she needs to do.
7. Pray for God to cultivate in her the heart of a warrior.
8. Pray for the passions and gifts that will help her carry out her calling.
9. Pray for a vibrant relationship with Christ, a heart on fire for Him.

10. Pray for her to seek God's approval over human approval, living for her audience of One.
11. Pray for the Lord to be *with* her and *in* her. Pray for her to have a deep awareness of His presence.
12. Pray for sensitivity to the Holy Spirit's nudgings.
13. Pray for great friends and strong, healthy relationships.
14. Pray for her friends and most trusted circle.
15. Pray for light to find light, especially as friend groups shift.
16. Pray for unhealthy relationships to be short-lived and to teach her lessons about better choices in the future.
17. Pray for her college roommates and future boyfriends. Ask God to bring positive influences into her life.
18. Pray for strong mentors, teachers, coaches, and encouragers who recognize her potential, cultivate her gifts, and help her achieve her goals.
19. Pray for role models to help her see who she wants to be.
20. Pray for her future husband (if marriage is in God's will). Pray for a man who loves the Lord first and her second. Pray for protection over him, especially against temptation.
21. Pray for a strong conscience shaped by the Holy Spirit.
22. Pray for conviction from the Holy Spirit.
23. Pray for her to seek help when she feels troubled or ashamed.
24. Pray for her guardian angel to protect her.
25. Pray for spiritual discernment and a radar for truth.
26. Pray for doors to close if an opportunity isn't from God.
27. Pray for the thwarting of any evil planned or plotted against her.
28. Pray for her to trust her gut instincts.
29. Pray for escapes from dark situations.
30. Pray for a heightened awareness of God's mercy.
31. Pray for her to extend God's grace and forgive those who have wronged her.

32. Pray for her to stand on God's promises, especially as she finds herself on shaky ground.

33. Pray for her small mistakes to come to light so they don't evolve into bigger mistakes.

34. Pray for God to reveal Himself as He pursues her, rescues her, and meets her where she is.

35. Pray for her to own her faith and stand firm in her convictions.

36. Pray for any seeds you plant now to take root at a time most opportune to her salvation.

37. Pray for humility, resilience, strength, stamina, a strong work ethic, courage, confidence, wisdom, clarity, fortitude, patience, perseverance, peace, and self-control.

38. Pray for her to use technology responsibly.

39. Pray for a thick skin and a tender heart, the ability to handle hard realities without letting them harden her.

40. Pray for a grateful spirit.

41. Pray for obedience to God.

42. Pray for God to bless the choices that honor Him.

43. Pray for her to become a good steward of her pain, sharing her testimony to help others.

44. Pray for new beginnings.

45. Pray for good career choices and strong mentors.

46. Pray for the souls she will impact and influence.

47. Pray for patience with God's plan.

48. Pray for her to live bravely and boldly for Jesus.

49. Pray for her to love the Lord with all her heart, mind, and soul.

50. Pray for her to finish strong and serve her purpose here on earth.

Max Lucado says, "Our prayers may be awkward. Our attempts may be feeble. But since the power of prayer is in the one who hears it and not the one who says it, our prayers do make a difference."[4]

God answers prayers, but He can't answer what we don't pray. Our daughters face enormous challenges, and they need our help fighting physical and spiritual battles.

Only God has known, since the beginning of time, who your daughter is, why she was born, and what she was born to do. He has a plan for her life that you're called to enable, not interrupt. Your daughter will impact thousands of people in her lifetime, and as you pray and empower her through faith, ask God to use her in big and small ways to make her a light for her generation and the generations that follow as she gets launched into the future.

Those who trust in the LORD will find new strength. They will soar high on wings like eagles. They will run and not grow weary. They will walk and not faint.

–ISAIAH 40:31 NLT

"HOPE IS ROOTED IN MEMORY"

One reason why teenagers struggle is because they don't have much history to draw on.

Unlike adults, who can look back on their lives and see examples of how heartaches and disappointments worked out, teenagers live in a world of *firsts*. They are feeling:

- Their first big rejection.
- Their first broken heart.
- Their first major failure.
- Their first crushing disappointment.
- Their first mistake they'll always regret.

- Their first setback that feels like punishment.
- Their first dream that doesn't come true.

Understandably, they may wonder if they'll survive. As Rod Stewart and Sheryl Crow both famously sang, the first cut is the deepest, and nobody forgets their first blow of real pain.

Yet God is faithful, and He carries us through storms. He is at work in our lives, even when we feel forgotten or overlooked. Faith is best understood in hindsight, and only as we look back on a trial can we see His presence and protection. Only upon reflection can we see how different pieces of the puzzle ultimately fit together.

Currently, your daughter has limited life experiences. She may have only a few examples of God helping her through hard times. By reminding her of who God is and what He has done in your life, her life, and Scripture, you help her connect the dots.

In the book *Boundaries*, the authors say the Bible is full of God's reminding His people of what He did in the past to give them faith for the future. "Hope is rooted in memory," they write. "We remember getting help in the past and that gives us hope for the future."[5]

Teenagers need hope, and since Jesus is the ultimate hope, they need Him. They need parents and mentors who empower them through faith and help them see today's trials as tomorrow's testimonies—stories of survival they will eventually share with their friends and future children.

It is up to every generation to equip the one behind them. As moms, we can pray for our daughters to outdo us. We can give them the tools and encouragement to dive deeper into their faith and draw more hearts to God than we did in our lifetime. We can pray that our ceiling becomes their floor and that any arrows they send into the future fly higher and farther than ours once did.

Our work as mothers matters. Our prayers have lifelong impact. Our daughters are in the hands of a God who knows them, loves them, and provides the ultimate security in their lives.

———————— • ————————

God is within her, she will not fall; God will help her at the break of day.

–PSALM 46:5

———————— • ————————

REFLECTION QUESTIONS

1. Name a terrifying time in your daughter's life when you realized your lack of control. How did it affect your faith?

2. On a scale of one to ten, how comfortable are you with prayer? Do you believe it makes a difference? Have you *seen* it make a difference? Do you doubt the power of your prayers or believe that other prayers are heard above yours? Explain.

3. What blessings in your life may have resulted from someone's prayers for you? Explain.

4. What trials did you face as a teenager that God carried you through? How has He worked in your daughter's trials? Does your daughter give God credit for His work in her life?

5. "The older our kids get, the more we go to God about our children than we go to our children about God." Do you agree? Why or why not?

6. Have you ever thought about your prayers outliving you? How does it change your prayer life knowing that you can impact a world you'll never see?

CONCLUSION

N*obody loves me like my mother.* I've thought this on many occasions, one being an event in my hometown after my first book was released.

My parents came to hear me speak to middle school girls. As I finished, I glanced in their direction, curious and nervous to gauge their reaction.

It wasn't my best talk—yet my mom's face said otherwise. She was beaming at me, proud as a peacock, with a grin the size of Texas. Any doubts I ever had about her love for me vanished because her expression offered proof.

Nobody loves me like my mother, and nobody beams at me like my mother when I make her proud.

I realize I am lucky. I know women who grew up with critical, narcissistic, or abusive mothers. I know parents who struggle to show love because they never saw love modeled. We all parent in response to how we were parented, yet even if your home life was a wreck, *you* can break the cycle. You can learn from your mom's example and decide who *you* want to become.

Your relationship with your daughter will constantly change.

That teenage girl who you wish would tell you everything may not be ready for that now, but as she ages and your relationship evolves into a friendship, the floodgates may open. You two may look back on your highs and lows—that time she made you prouder than a peacock, that time you considered disowning her—and laugh hysterically.

And when your daughter is thirty, she may randomly call you—like my friend who called her mother—to say, "I'm so sorry, Mom." It may hit her, as she's out shopping and sees a teenage girl acting surly toward her mom, how she once did that. In these moments her affection toward you may swell as she realizes that even at her worst, you never gave up on her.

Because nobody loves a girl like her mother.

I know you feel totally unequipped some days. You may constantly ask, *Is this the right choice? Should I let her go? Is this a fight worth fighting? How do I love her* and *discipline her? Why does doing the right thing make me feel alone? Why is my daughter pulling away and shutting down? What am I doing wrong? Will our relationship ever feel warm again?*

If parenting came with a crystal ball, our decisions would be easy. We could confidently make choices today to achieve the outcome we dream of tomorrow.

Clearly, it doesn't work that way, and that is good for our faith because if we had every answer up front, we wouldn't need God. We'd never be humbled into listening to Him, leaning on Him, and opening our hearts to His wisdom.

God is crazy about you, and as He pursues your heart, He waits patiently for you to respond. When you do respond, and when you open your heart to Jesus, He gives you the Holy Spirit. He pours down love and grace so you can share them with others.

This lets you pursue your daughter's heart and model our Father's love in visible, earthly ways.

The same God who helps you raise your daughter also works in her heart. He covers your relationship from many angles, aiming for unity. Even if your home feels more like a battleground than a holy ground—when the only anthem you hear is slammed doors or the silent treatment—there is hope. God is still writing the story about you and your daughter.

Today's chapter is the teen years, and while the world revels in a juicy mother-daughter catfight, I challenge you to think bigger. Accept God's love for you, and then let it inspire your parenting. Ask Him to work in your relationship as you apply the ten ideas of this book:

1. Choose your words (and timing) carefully.
2. Listen and empathize with her world.
3. Be her mom.
4. Make your relationship a priority.
5. See the good, loving her *as* she is and *where* she is.
6. Help her find good friends and positive influences.
7. Be her emotional coach.
8. Enjoy her, laugh often, and have fun.
9. Take care of yourself and have a support system for hard days.
10. Pray for her and empower her through faith.

Once again, God handpicked *you* to raise your daughter. You are the perfect imperfect woman for the job. Even when you hit a new low, even when you're crying on your closet floor and seeking new direction, He is present. His power is made perfect in weakness, and through your most vulnerable moments, you'll experience the depth of His kindness and mercy.

You'll learn that God is, indeed, real.

So be kind to yourself, kind to your daughter, and kind to

your fellow moms. Remember that we are on the same team, because what is good for one girl is good for all girls. A win for one mom is a win for all moms. Invest in your family, yet look outside your family too. Find women you trust to cheer you on, pick you up, and keep your spirits high.

As for your teenage daughter—give praise. Thank God for this lifelong sister of the heart. The next time you see her, hug her just because. Tell your daughter you've been thinking about her and you want her to know how very grateful you are that God chose you to be her mom.

———————— ● ————————

I thank my God every time I remember you.

–PHILIPPIANS 1:3

———————— ● ————————

ACKNOWLEDGMENTS

Here in the South, where college football is king, there exists one of the most famous rivalries in sports: Alabama versus Auburn.

I am a lifelong Alabama fan, yet the idea for this book was birthed in the heart of Auburn country. The irony of this fact reminds me that God does, indeed, have a sense of humor.

I was invited by Drew Speakman to speak at a back-to-school event for mothers and daughters at FUMC Opelika. After delivering the keynote address, I spoke to the moms separately. My talk was titled "How to Love a Teenager," and it was a message I always enjoyed sharing because it allowed me to admit some failures that led to my best parenting lessons.

After the talk, several women came up on stage to share their personal stories. One Southern woman (whose name I regrettably don't know) walked up, pointed at me, and boldly declared, "*That* needs to be your next book!"

Immediately, the lightbulb flashed in my head. The clouds cleared, and after years of waiting for a new book idea to grab me, I finally had an answer. Since I'm a slow writer, I've learned to be patient and careful with what I commit to. I know from experience that I'll spend one year writing a book and another year talking about it, so any topic I choose must ignite a fire in me.

Thankfully, the mother-teen daughter relationship did that. It was a subject that I could easily wrap my heart, mind, and arms around. For the next eight months after that event, I threw myself into a manuscript that quickly became a labor of love. The deeper I dove, the more I realized how much *I* needed the conversations I hoped to begin.

So to the woman in Opelika who fanned a flicker of an idea into a flame—I thank you. God spoke profoundly through you that day, and I'll always be grateful that you acted on His nudge to reveal my next book.

I also want to thank every mom who has bought *Liked* or *10 Ultimate Truths Girls Should Know* for their daughter or brought their daughter to a speaking event. Having a voice in your daughter's life is an amazing honor I don't take for granted, and this book is my love letter to *you*. For years you have inspired me with your stories, your questions, and the love I witness on your face as you smile at your daughter or describe her to me. Even during the trials of adolescence, you love your daughter passionately, and your commitment to help her—and find tools that help you— fuels my hope for the future.

To my agent, Andrew Wolgemuth, who takes on new roles with each new book. Andrew, I can always count on you for sound judgment, solid advice, wisdom, legal interpretation, timely responses, and advocacy. You lead well, with your trademark integrity and humility, and I'd be lost trying to navigate the world of publishing without you. Thank you for handling the business end of matters so I can create and dream. I'm lucky to be part of your team and benefit from the collective wisdom of Wolgemuth & Associates.

To my brother, Jack Kubiszyn, who is never too busy to take his sister's call. Thank you for guiding me, looking out for me, and offering diligent legal counsel. You're the best brother on the planet, and I love you.

To Megan Dobson, who brought this book to the W team and set the wheels in motion. Thank you for your enthusiasm, editing, and belief in the message. I should have known we'd be fast friends once we realized our common interest. (Roll Tide!)

To Beth Adams, whose encouragement and leadership during the final stage of editing prepared this book to launch. I'm so glad I got to work with you, and I'll always remember fondly our fun lunch in New York.

To Dawn Hollomon, whose meticulous attention to detail and thoughtful edits polished the manuscript beautifully, and to the phenomenal team at W Publishing Group/Thomas Nelson: Stephanie Newton, Debbie Wickwire, Damon Reiss, Sara Broun, Ashley Reed, Caren Wolfe, Katherine Hudencial, Allison Carter, and the marketing and publicity teams. You quickly caught the vision for *Love Her Well* and fostered a collaboration. Thank you for being a talented, hardworking, and dedicated team. This book is in great hands as you steward it into the world.

To my priest, Father Bob Sullivan, for reviewing the manuscript from a faith perspective. And to my friend and first reader, Kimberly Powell, for elevating the manuscript to the next level with every suggestion, rearranged chapter, and story in the margin. Your skills are unmatched, and I'm so blessed to benefit from your many talents and generous spirit.

To the prayer warriors who influenced this book, especially Beth Lawrence, Julie Butler, Jennifer Gray, Liz Blalock, Shannon Thomas, LeAnn McMillan, and Julie Gillis. Thank you for speaking truth, calming my anxieties, and always being game for a deep conversation.

To YiaYia and Papou, my Greek mother-in-law and late father-in-law, whose culture of loving your family well has taught me so much about showing up and engaging in your children's lives even after they leave the nest. People often wonder what you did to raise three great children who adore each other as siblings, and I know it began with your values and choices as a family. Thank you for loving me like one of your own. Papou, we sure do miss you.

To my mother and father, Lucy and Jack Kubiszyn, who loved me well when I least deserved it, even when I acted moody or made choices that disappointed you. You never withdrew your love or worried about how my behavior reflected on you as parents. Instead, you cared about *me*. You put my well-being and my relationship with God above all things, and you believed in me with a passion that gave me the courage to dream and the reassurance of having a soft place to land. Thank you for your unconditional love, your prayers, and the four siblings you gave me—Mary Kathryn, Jack, Dana, and Krissie—to be my lifelong friends.

To my daughters, Ella, Sophie, Marie Claire, and Camille. Being your mom is the greatest honor of my life, and nothing compares to the joy that you girls bring your daddy and me. I'm so proud of each of you, and I hope that one day, when you're a mother or a mentor, you'll read this book and feel encouraged. You girls are my heart, and I thank God that I get to accompany you in each new season of your journey.

To Harry, whose quiet strength gives wind to my sails. You are my best friend, my sounding board, and my shock absorber when life gets tough. We both know that I couldn't do this job without you—not only because of your commitment as a husband and father, but also because of your emotional and moral support. Thank you for listening to me, wiping tears, and inspiring me to be a better person. Only God could have given me the sense at twenty-two years old to recognize what a great life partner you'd make, and now that we're getting gray and old together, I realize how instrumental that decision was. I love you always.

And to Christ my Savior, the ultimate source of strength and the root of anything that goes well. I fail daily, yet through you, I have the peace and comfort of knowing the best is yet to come. There is eternal hope and a grace that is bigger than any regret or mistake on earth. Writing can be lonely work, yet you're faithfully beside me, helping me press on. I ask that you bless the moms who read this book and lift them out of discouragement. Fill them with a spirit of strength and flood their homes with joy and love. To God be the honor and glory.

NOTES

Introduction

1. Dr. Gary Chapman, *The 5 Love Languages of Teenagers* (Chicago, IL: Northfield Publishing, 2000, 2005, 2010), 14.
2. Carol Kuykendall and Krista Gilbert, *Give Them Wings* (Carol Stream, IL: A Focus on the Family Resource Published by Tyndale House Publishers, 1994, 2018), xx–xxi.
3. C. S. Lewis, *Mere Christianity* (New York, NY: HarperCollins Publishers, 1952, 1980), 141.

Chapter 1: Choose Your Words (and Timing) Carefully

1. Alice Churnock, "Leave the Cowlick Alone: The Art of Effective Criticism," Rooted Ministry website, September 25, 2018, accessed April 30, 2019, from https://www.rootedministry.com /blog/leave-the-cowlick-alone-the-art-of-effective-criticism/.
2. Mark Batterson, *Whisper* (Colorado Springs, CO: Multnomah Publishers, 2017), 189.
3. Sissy Goff, David Thomas, and Melissa Trevathan, *Intentional Parenting* (Nashville, TN: Thomas Nelson, 2013), 153.
4. William Barclay in Joanna Weaver, *Having a Mary Heart in a Martha World* (Colorado Springs, CO: Waterbrook Press, 2000, 2002), 166.
5. Geri Scazzero, *The Emotionally Healthy Woman* (Grand Rapids, MI: Zondervan, 2010), 79.

6. Dr. Gary Chapman, *The 5 Love Languages of Teenagers* (Chicago, IL: Northfield Publishing, 2000, 2005, 2010), 47–48.

Chapter 2: Listen and Empathize with Her World

1. Dr. Stephen R. Covey quote, accessed April 30, 2019, from https://www.franklincovey.com/the-7-habits/habit-5.html.

2. Amy Ellis Nutt, "Why Kids and Teens Face Far More Anxiety These Days," *The Washington Post*, May 10, 2018, accessed April 30, 2019, from https://www.washingtonpost.com/news /to-your-health/wp/2018/05/10/why-kids-and-teens-may-face -far-more-anxiety-these-days/?noredirect=on&utm_term =.352fb2063b2d.

3. Dr. Lisa Damour, website accessed April 30, 2019, from https:// www.drlisadamour.com/under-pressure/.

4. John Portch, "Inside the Alabama Crimson Tide," Leaders, July 23, 2018, https://leadersinsport.com/performance/inside -alabama-crimson-tide/.

5. Jane O'Donnell and Shari Rudavsky, "Young Americans Are the Loneliest, Surprising Study from Cigna Shows," USA Today Network, May 1, 2018, updated September 6, 2018, https://www .usatoday.com/story/news/politics/2018/05/01/loneliness-poor -health-reported-far-more-among-young-people-than-even -those-over-72/559961002/.

6. Jean M. Twenge, "Have Smartphones Destroyed a Generation?" *The Atlantic*, September 2017, https://www.theatlantic.com /magazine/archive/2017/09/has-the-smartphone-destroyed-a -generation/534198/.

7. Fiza Pirani, "The Suicide Rate for Teen Girls Is the Highest It's Been in 40 Years—Is Social Media to Blame?" *Atlanta Journal-Constitution*, August 4, 2017, https://www.ajc.com/news/national /the-suicide-rate-for-teen-girls-the-highest-been-years-social -media-blame/2gJQWzLABx1ItVZroM5MCO/.

8. Twenge, "Have Smartphones Destroyed a Generation?"

9. Frances E. Jensen, *The Teenage Brain* (New York: HarperCollins, 2015), 220.

10. Jensen, 211–12.

11. Michele Borba, APB Speakers, accessed April 30, 2019, https://www.apbspeakers.com/speaker/michele-borba/.

12. Madeline Levine, *Teach Your Children Well* (New York: HarperCollins, 2012), 108–9.

13. Jensen, *The Teenage Brain*, 104–5.

14. Jensen, 104–5.

15. Meg Meeker, *Strong Fathers, Strong Daughters* (New York: Ballantine Books, 2007), 206.

16. Francis X. Rocca, "Pope Says 'Throwaway Culture' Harms Environment and Human Life," *Catholic News Service*, June 5, 2013, https://www.catholicnews.com/services/englishnews/2013/pope-says-throwaway-culture-harms-environment-and-human-life.cfm; Patricia Garcia, "11 Pieces of Relationship Advice We Learned from Pope Francis," *Vogue*, April 8, 2016, https://www.vogue.com/article/pope-francis-amoris-laetitia-relationship-advice; Agence France-Presse, "Pope Francis: I Have Felt Used by the 'Friends' I Make in This Job," *Guardian*, September 15, 2015, https://www.theguardian.com/world/2015/sep/15/pope-francis-i-have-felt-used-by-fake-friends.

17. Carol S. Dweck, *Mindset* (New York: Ballantine Books, 2016), 7.

18. Jensen, *The Teenage Brain*, 109.

19. Jensen, 114.

20. C. S. Lewis, *Mere Christianity* (1952; repr., New York: HarperCollins, 1980), 136–37.

Chapter 3: Be Her Mom

1. Henry Cloud and John Townsend, *Boundaries* (Grand Rapids: Zondervan, 1992), 198.

2. Rick Warren, *The Purpose Driven Life: What on Earth Am I Here For?* (Grand Rapids: Zondervan, 2012), 48.

3. Frances E. Jensen, *The Teenage Brain* (New York: HarperCollins, 2015), 269.

4. Jensen, 12–13.

5. Jensen, 103–4.

6. Jensen, 23.

7. Jensen, 64.

8. Jensen, 203–4.

9. Jensen, 168.

10. Jensen, 13.

11. Sissy Goff, David Thomas, and Melissa Trevathan, *Intentional Parenting* (Nashville: Thomas Nelson, 2013), 205.

12. Foster Cline and Jim Fay, *Parenting Teens with Love and Logic* (Colorado Springs: NavPress, 2006), 24.

13. Carol S. Dweck, *Mindset* (New York: Ballantine Books, 2016), 200.

14. Warren, *The Purpose Driven Life*, 202.

15. Meg Meeker, *Strong Fathers, Strong Daughters* (New York: Ballantine Books, 2007), 218.

16. Cloud and Townsend, *Boundaries*, 36.

17. Cloud and Townsend, 112.

18. Lisa Damour, *Under Pressure* (New York: Ballantine Books, 2019), xvi.

19. The Healthy Teen Project, accessed April 30, 2019, http://www.healthyteenproject.com/adolescent-eating-disorders-ca.

20. Lisa Damour, *Untangled* (New York: Ballantine Books, 2016), 118.

21. Jensen, *The Teenage Brain*, 127.

22. Damour, *Untangled*, 263.

23. Jensen, *The Teenage Brain*, 162–3.

24. Cloud and Townsend, *Boundaries*, 198–99.

25. Goff, Thomas, and Trevathan, *Intentional Parenting*, 66.

26. Goff, Thomas, and Trevathan, 204.

27. Damour, *Untangled*, 128–29.

28. Gary Chapman, *The 5 Love Languages of Teenagers* (Chicago: Northfield, 2010), 147.

29. Andrew C. Pearson Jr., "A Word from the Dean," *Adventurer* (Newsletter of the Cathedral Church of the Advent, Birmingham, AL), February 24, 2019, 1.

30. Joseph V. Corpora, *The Relentless Mercy of God* (Notre Dame, IN: Corby Books, 2017), 82.

Chapter 4: Make Your Relationship a Priority

1. Matt Mayberry, "What Truly Matters Most in Life and in the Game of Business," *Entrepreneur*, June 26, 2015, https://www.entrepreneur.com/article/247777.

2. Sissy Goff and Melissa Trevathan, *The Back Door to Your Teen's Heart* (BookSurge, 2007), 17.

3. Mother Angelica and Raymond Arroyo, *Mother Angelica's Little Book of Life Lessons and Everyday Spirituality* (New York: Doubleday, 2007), 140.

4. Frances E. Jensen, *The Teenage Brain* (New York: HarperCollins, 2015), 10.

5. Lisa Damour, *Untangled* (New York: Ballantine Books, 2016), 126.

6. Jonathan "JP" Pokluda, *Welcome to Adulting* (Grand Rapids: Baker, 2018), 113.

7. Damour, *Untangled*, 21–24.

Chapter 5: See the Good, Loving Her as She Is and Where She Is

1. Henry Cloud and John Townsend, *Boundaries* (Grand Rapids: Zondervan, 1992), 48.

2. Michelangelo, "Quotes of Michelangelo," accessed April 30, 2019, https://www.michelangelo.org/michelangelo-quotes.jsp.

3. Sissy Goff and Melissa Trevathan, *The Back Door to Your Teen's Heart* (BookSurge, 2007), 52.

4. Joanna Weaver, *Having a Mary Heart in a Martha World* (Colorado Springs: Waterbrook, 2002), 152.

5. Kathryn Stockett, "You Is Smart, You Is Kind, You Is Important," *The Help*, YouTube, October 14, 2011, https://www.youtube.com /watch?v=3H50llsHm3k.

6. Frances E. Jensen, *The Teenage Brain* (New York: HarperCollins, 2015), 37.

7. Jensen, 26–27.

8. Anne Lamott, quoted in Max Lucado, *Grace* (Nashville: Thomas Nelson, 2012), 145.

9. "A Mighty Girl on Facebook," accessed April 30, 2019, https:// www.facebook.com/amightygirl/posts/girls-self-esteem-peaks -at-9-years-old-42-of-1st-3rd-grade-girls-want-to-be-thin /955213457848301/.

Chapter 6: Help Her Find Good Friends and Positive Influences

1. Lisa Damour, *Untangled* (New York: Ballantine Books, 2016), 48.

2. Liz Mineo, "Good Genes Are Nice, but Joy Is Better," *Harvard Gazette*, April 11, 2017, https://news.harvard.edu/gazette/story /2017/04/over-nearly-80-years-harvard-study-has-been-showing -how-to-live-a-healthy-and-happy-life/.

3. Damour, *Untangled*, 81.

4. Meg Meeker, *Strong Fathers, Strong Daughters* (New York: Ballantine Books, 2007), 79.

Chapter 7: Be Her Emotional Coach

1. Lisbeth Splawn, "How to Raise an Emotionally Healthy Daughter," Meg Meeker MD, February 8, 2019, from https://www .megmeekermd.com/blog/how-to-raise-an-emotionally-healthy -daughter/.

2. Lisa Damour, *Untangled* (New York: Ballantine Books, 2016), 100–1.

3. Frances E. Jensen, *The Teenage Brain* (New York: HarperCollins, 2015), 170–71.

4. Splawn, "How to Raise an Emotionally Healthy Daughter."

Chapter 8: Enjoy Her, Laugh Often, and Have Fun

1. Sissy Goff, David Thomas, and Melissa Trevathan, *Intentional Parenting* (Nashville: Thomas Nelson, 2013), 204.

2. Hal Hinson, "Steel Magnolias," *Washington Post*, November 17, 1989, https://www.washingtonpost.com/wp-srv/style/longterm/movies/videos/steelmagnolias.htm.

3. Sissy Goff and Melissa Trevathan, *The Back Door to Your Teen's Heart* (BookSurge, 2007), 113–14.

4. C. S. Lewis, *The Screwtape Letters* (1942; repr., New York: HarperOne, 1996), 75–79.

Chapter 9: Take Care of Yourself and Have a Support System for Hard Days

1. Madeline Levine, *Teach Your Children Well* (New York: HarperCollins, 2012), 179.

2. Lysa TerKeurst, "Bad Moments Don't Make Bad Moms," Proverbs 31 Ministries, April 12, 2018, https://www.proverbs31.org/read/devotions/full-post/2018/04/12/bad-moments-dont-make-bad-moms.

3. Henry Cloud and John Townsend, *Boundaries* (Grand Rapids: Zondervan, 1992), 228.

4. Henri J. M. Nouwen, *The Return of the Prodigal Son* (New York: Doubleday, 1992), 119, 124.

5. Levine, *Teach Your Children Well*, 38.

6. Sissy Goff, David Thomas, and Melissa Trevathan, *Intentional Parenting* (Nashville: Thomas Nelson, 2013), 218.

Chapter 10: Pray for Her and Empower Her Through Faith

1. Meg Meeker, *Strong Fathers, Strong Daughters* (New York: Ballantine Books, 2007), 183.

2. Roy Baldwin, "Prayer: Seek the Lord Together," Focus on the Family, January 1, 2012, https://www.focusonthefamily.com /parenting/parenting-roles/dads-make-every-day-count/prayer -seek-the-lord-together.

3. Cameron Cole, "Mystery and Lament: When It Looks Like Your Child's Life Is Falling Apart," Rooted Ministry, January 13, 2017, https://www.rootedministry.com/blog/mystery-lament-looks -like-childs-life-falling-apart/.

4. Max Lucado, "Our Prayers Do Make a Difference," Crosswalk.com, October 20, 2003, https://www.crosswalk.com /faith/spiritual-life/our-prayers-do-make-a-difference-1225673 .html.

5. Henry Cloud and John Townsend, *Boundaries* (Grand Rapids: Zondervan, 1992), 267.

ABOUT THE AUTHOR

Kari Kubiszyn Kampakis is an author, blogger, and national speaker from Birmingham, Alabama. Her books for teen girls, *10 Ultimate Truths Girls Should Know* and *Liked: Whose Approval Are You Living For?*, have been used widely across the country by teen youth groups and church groups to empower girls through faith.

Kari's work has been featured on the *Today* show, *Today Parents*, Yahoo! News, EWTN, Proverbs 31, Ann Voskamp's blog, The Huffington Post, and other national outlets. She also hosts a new podcast called *Girl Mom*. She and her husband, Harry, have four daughters and a dog named Lola. Learn more by visiting www.karikampakis.com or finding Kari on Facebook, Instagram, Pinterest, and Twitter.